SOUTH WEST AFRICA
An International Problem

SOUTH WEST AFRICA

An International Problem

R. W. IMISHUE

Issued under the auspices of the
Institute of Race Relations, London

PALL MALL PRESS

LONDON

Published by
PALL MALL PRESS
77–79 Charlotte Street, London W1
and Dunmow, Essex

First published 1965

© 1965 Institute of Race Relations

Printed by Butler and Tanner Ltd, Frome and London

CONTENTS

Foreword *by Philip Mason*   vii
Map: South West Africa and her Neighbours   viii

1 The Establishment of the Mandate   1
2 The Administration of the Trust under the League
   of Nations   7
3 South West Africa and Union–German Relations   15
4 From the League to the United Nations   20
5 South West Africa and the United Nations 1946–53   28
6 South West Africa and the United Nations 1953–61   40
7 A New Era: From 1960   55

Appendix I: Article 22 of the League of Nations Covenant   64
Appendix II: The Mandate for South West Africa   66
*Appendix III: United Nations Charter. Chapter XII: Inter-
   national Trusteeship System, Articles 75–80*   69
Select Bibliography   72
References   74

FOREWORD

I⊤ seems at the time of writing that there is some likelihood of the judgment of the International Court regarding South West Africa being handed down in the autumn of 1965. If so, there will be a number of people anxious to understand the background to the judgment and when the Institute of Race Relations heard that Dr Imishue had completed a doctoral thesis on the subject of South West Africa, we were anxious to see it and to publish it as near as we could to the time the judgment was expected.

The thesis, however, was long and not entirely suited to our needs. It contained much material which was fascinating in itself and of permanent value to scholars, but not all having direct bearing on the present position of South West Africa in world affairs.

We therefore proposed to him that the scope of his work should be considerably reduced and limited to this special interest. To this he generously agreed and the work of editing and abridging has been carried out by Mrs Cleodie Mackinnon.

PHILIP MASON

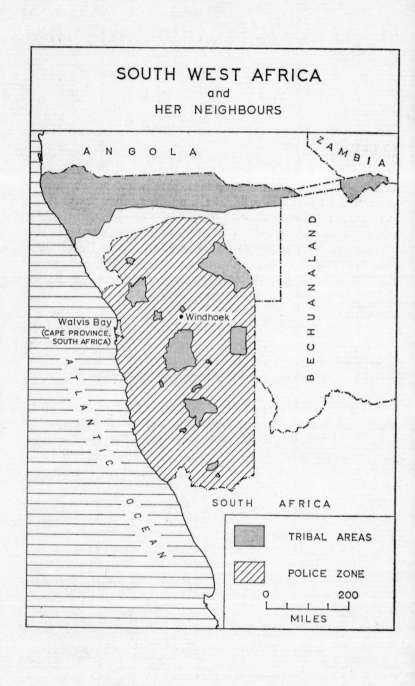

SOUTH WEST AFRICA
and
HER NEIGHBOURS

ANGOLA

ZAMBIA

BECHUANALAND

Walvis Bay
(CAPE PROVINCE,
SOUTH AFRICA)

• Windhoek

ATLANTIC

OCEAN

SOUTH   AFRICA

TRIBAL AREAS

POLICE ZONE

0   200

MILES

I

THE ESTABLISHMENT OF THE MANDATE

INTERNATIONAL concern with South West Africa begins with its acquisition by Germany as a colonial possession in 1883. But, in 1915, after a brief triumphant campaign, the forces of the Union of South Africa, led by Generals Smuts and Botha, conquered the area. Most South Africans hoped for annexation of the territory by the Union. South West Africa, they felt, was South Africa's by right of conquest; by the end of the war it had, moreover, been peacefully administered by her for four years. Ties with the Union, both personal and economic, were strong: even under German rule there had been, in 1914, 2,000 South African settlers and much South African capital in the territory. Germany's presence there, South Africans felt, had been allowed only by British lukewarmness: this potential extension of the Union went by default when the German Government received no reply, in 1883, to its inquiry concerning British suzerainty over the area where a German trader operated. Thus Germany gained sovereignty from the Orange River to the Angolan frontier. The port of Walvis Bay, however (South West Africa's only port of commercial importance), remained, as it still is, an integral part of the Cape Province.

The Union wanted control of South West Africa, not because of any economic potential (little was apparent in the huge semi-desert territory) but because it constituted a security risk. Minor German military installations had been found there; it had fostered dissidence among Union nationals, and it provided, as it may still provide, a potential base for hostile activities against South Africa.

The disposition of South West Africa, however, was not in the hands of the Union. She had conquered the territory in the Allied cause, and it was for the Allies, at the Peace Conference of 1919, to decide its future. The Allies were, on the whole, sympathetic towards the idea of annexation, but for various reasons it was found to be politically impracticable. Their main objectives in the settlement of all colonies were:

(1) Protection of the interests of the indigenous peoples, which were held to be paramount.

(2) Establishment of a system of tutelage to ensure this protection.

(3) Non-annexation of ex-enemy colonies.

(4) Expression of the settlement reached in formal legal terms.

South West Africa could not be treated differently from the other colonies. The Allies were to some extent bound by their own non-annexationist propaganda during the war, but were limited even more by the fifth of President Wilson's Fourteen Points in his programme for peace. This called for

> . . . a free, open-minded and absolutely impartial adjustment of all colonial claims, based upon a strict observance of the principle that in determining all such questions of sovereignty, the interests of the populations concerned must have equal weight with the equitable claims of the Government whose title is to be determined.[1]

This was fairly soon interpreted to mean that

> . . . a colonial Power acts not as owner of its colonies, but as trustee for the nations and for the interests of the Society of Nations, that the terms on which the colonial administration is conducted are a matter of international concern and may legitimately be the subject of international inquiry and that the Peace Conference may, therefore, write a code of colonial conduct binding upon all colonial Powers.[2]

This interpretation is a clear departure from the idea of sovereign title over colonies as stated in Point Five, but was later approved by Wilson as a satisfactory interpretation of the principles involved,[3] and was apparently also used at the Conference.[4] Wilson repeatedly condemned imperialistic motives and supported the principle of self-determination and the protection of

2

the interests of weaker peoples, seeking for the reign of law, based on the consent of the governed.[5] He envisaged a settlement based on conceptions of international justice, and the Allies were fully committed to his non-annexationist principles; but his proposals at this stage were largely negative, and it cannot be said that they committed the Allied Powers in advance to the acceptance of the mandate principle.

A number of alternatives faced the Peace Conference in disposing of all Germany's colonies. Annexation, as we have seen, was ruled out because of the Allies' commitment to President Wilson's proposals. The Allies were unanimous that none of the colonies should be returned to Germany, who in their view stood convicted of maladministration of colonial possessions. Independence was not at that time a practicable alternative, as the colonial peoples were not sufficiently advanced. International administration, originally proposed by President Wilson in his Paris draft,[6] was widely opposed among the Allies as being impracticable for a number of reasons, from cumbrousness to confusion.

The compromise solution which emerged was the system of international mandates, which bridged the gap between Wilson's ideals and the annexationist demands of some of the Allies at the Peace Conference. It had some sort of precedent in various international agreements and proposals during the previous fifty years, which had modified the usual colonial relationships in favour of the internationally guaranteed protection of backward races; for example, in the Powers' guarantee in 1887 of the Congo's independence, assigning its government to Leopold II; in the proposal in 1898 for a Central Powers mandate over Crete; and, within the British Empire, the Imperial Government's assignment to Australia of the administration of Papua; the idea of trusteeship had been current since Burke's speeches on Fox's India Bill,[7] and had been used by the United States to justify her administration of the Philippines.[8] Mandates had first been suggested in a scheme proposed by Smuts himself for the territories formerly owned by Russia, Turkey, Austria and Hungary, which stressed the principles of self-determination and trusteeship, and the supervisory powers and ultimate control of the League of Nations.[9] But he had never

3

envisaged its application to Germany's colonies in Africa, which he regarded as too backward for the principle of self-determination to be applicable.[10] Like other British Dominions who had conquered enemy territory, South Africa favoured annexation; in this she had the support of M. Simon, French Minister for Colonies, and of Lloyd George, though the latter had admitted the wishes and interests of the native inhabitants to be paramount. But Wilson was fascinated by the idea of a mandate, which he felt to be ethically desirable and compatible with his programme for peace;[11] he was determined, as the Allies were committed, against annexation.

The central idea of the mandate system was therefore embodied in the first paragraph of Article 22 of the League of Nations Covenant (reproduced in full in Appendix I):

> To those colonies and territories which as a consequence of the late war have ceased to be under the sovereignty of the States which formerly governed them and which are inhabited by peoples not yet able to stand by themselves under the strenuous conditions of the modern world, there should be applied the principle that the well-being and development of such peoples form a sacred trust of civilization. . . .

All that the annexationists could salvage at this stage was the classification of the mandated territories into categories—A, B and C—on the basis of the stage of development of the inhabitants, and other circumstances such as economic conditions and geographical location. For 'A' mandates independence was in sight; these were communities formerly belonging to the Turkish Empire. 'B' mandates were former German colonies, especially those of Central Africa, to be administered as separate entities from the mandatory power. 'C' mandates were to be administered under the laws of the mandatory as integral parts of its territory. Into this class South West Africa fell.

Further paragraphs of the Article included other ideals of the system such as the accountability of the mandatory power for the administration of its trust, and the international supervision of the trust to ensure observance of its terms.

The 'C' class mandates, including South West Africa, were distributed by the Supreme Council in May 1919. In principle it should have been the League of Nations Council, taking

4

cognizance of the Supreme Council's allocation, who notified the mandatory powers of their appointment and the terms of the mandates. Actually, since the question of the colonial settlement arose before the Covenant was drafted or the Council of the League formed, it was the Principal Allied and Associated Powers who implemented it, as it had been to them that German sovereignty had been relinquished. It has therefore been suggested that association with these powers, rather than League title, is important in the mandate system.[12]

All the conquerors retained the territories of their conquest, not as spoils of war but as mandates to be administered on behalf of the League. Framing of mandate charters or agreements was left to the mandatory powers, with the stipulation that they be in the spirit of Article 22 of the Covenant.

South Africa had first asked the Council of Ten (a steering committee composed of representatives of the five Principal Allied Powers) that South West Africa be incorporated in the Union. She based her claim on the close economic and political ties between the two territories, on her own security requirements and on the fact that she had actually occupied and administered South West Africa for four years. It was a claim which was regarded with sympathy in many quarters; Lloyd George supported and even expected eventual incorporation, and even Wilson did not reject it out of hand, but said it must wait 'until the day when the true wishes of the inhabitants could be ascertained. It was up to the Union of South Africa to make it so attractive that South West Africa would come to the Union of its own free will'.[13]

So the Union only obtained a 'C' class mandate over South West Africa. She was thus classed among 'advanced nations who by reason of their resources, their experience or their geographical position, can best undertake this responsibility', of the tutelage of the natives of the territory. It was hence argued, by the Portuguese representative on the Mandates Commission, Mr Freire d'Andrade, that the mandate would not have been assigned to South Africa if her system of laws and the general principles which it applied had been unsatisfactory; they were already clear in the Boer constitution of the Transvaal and Orange Free State, which said 'In church and state, there is no equality between black and white'.[14] No such test, however, was applied at Versailles in the distribution of the mandates: the only criteria were conquest and contiguity.

Article 22 was criticized for vagueness, and for being couched in rhetorical and argumentative rather than legislative language;[15] this reflects its origin of compromise. It has left the door open to controversy on such topics as the ultimate goal for mandated territories. Because an end to the mandates is not provided for in the Article (except in the case of 'A' class mandates) it has been argued that independence was not envisaged,[16] that 'the mandate is essentially final and perpetual'.[17] These views derive some support from the defeat in the Permanent Mandates Commission[18] of a proposal providing for proclamation of the independence of a mandate in due time.[19]

But many scholars still contend that mandates are temporary in character, basing their stand on the principles of non-annexation and self-determination behind the Peace Treaties of which the mandate system was a part, as well as on the phraseology of Article 22: the word 'mandate' itself and such expressions as 'peoples not yet able to stand by themselves', 'sacred trust', 'tutelage', 'safeguards in the interests of indigenous population', all of which seem to point to the eventual emancipation of the peoples under the régime.

Most of the League members, especially Italy, Germany, Spain, India and Haiti, held that all mandates were temporary, while most of the mandatory powers thought otherwise.[20] It seemed, however, likely that in the final analysis it would be the special circumstances of the territory and the existing international political situation, rather than legal arguments, which would determine the mandates' future.

2

THE ADMINISTRATION OF THE TRUST
UNDER THE LEAGUE OF NATIONS

THE mandate compromise embodied in the Covenant of the
League of Nations has not been interpreted authoritatively. The
ambiguity and obscurity of the wording of Article 22 caused
from the start an element of uncertainty in the South West
Africa question; the Permanent Mandates Commission[1] entrusted with the supervision of the mandate had only vague
and inadequate directives at its disposal, and had to fill in the
gaps from its members' conception of the spirit of the system. It
relied, for support and enforcement of its decisions, upon public
opinion; the emphasis therefore was on persuasion rather than
coercion, the result generally slow progress in a friendly
atmosphere. The actual means of pressure open to the Permanent Mandates Commission were the provision concerning
the remission of petitions from the inhabitants of South West
Africa, the annual report, and the publicizing of the discussions
of the Commission, and of its reports, to the League Council.

South Africa's authority as the mandatory power in South
West Africa rested on various legal and international instruments: Article 22 of the League of Nations Covenant, certain
other articles of the Treaty of Versailles,[2] the mandate charter
for South West Africa and subsequent rulings and interpreta-
tions of these documents by relevant organs of the League such
as the Permanent Mandates Commission and League Council.
The mandate charter lays down the basic laws of administration, and a legal analogy drawn between this and a contract in
national law led to South Africa's contention in 1950 that the

7

mandate lapsed with the demise of the League, one of the contracting parties. But the International Court of Justice pronounced this to be a false analogy;[3] the mandate system was an entirely new institution with new duties and obligations. These, however, in the absence of an accepted international standard of colonial administration, were never clearly defined.

The 'sacred trust of civilization', for which under Article 22 the mandatory power was responsible, was the issue on which most differences of opinion and interpretation arose. The 'material and moral welfare' of the populations of mandated territory was the pivot of the mandate system, and South Africa in repeated declarations in the League and elsewhere accepted her responsibility for this under the provisions of the mandate.[4] Most members of the League and Mandates Commission, in their conception of the sacred trust, put a very high premium on the interests of the native inhabitants, and almost excluded from consideration the welfare of the white population, who were presumed to be able to stand alone. The Union wanted to develop the territory as a good home for all elements in the population; to achieve this object she felt that very rapid progress for the white population was a top priority, so that the natives, the vast majority of whom were uncivilized, might learn from them. The native was to be inspired with respect for the civilization of the white man.[5]

South Africa's position found some support from the Portuguese representative on the Mandates Commission, who felt that methods of administration of mandates could differ in accordance with local conditions; they must always ensure equitable treatment of all the population, irrespective of race or colour.[6] The civilized race, he felt, might be allowed dominance. Other members of the Commission, however, limited the phrase 'not yet able to stand by themselves' to the native inhabitants, and stressed the difference from the colonial situation, against which, with its usual advocacy of white supremacy as the solution of the problems of relations between advanced and backward peoples, the mandates system was indeed a kind of protest. The white minority was here to be considered only in the context of protection of the native inhabitants.

The 'sacred trust' is thus seen to be a moral and political question, interpreted by the parties concerned in terms of their political philosophy and social attitudes. The difficulties of interpretation in relation to South West Africa hinge on the fact that this was the only mandate in which the interests of two races were seen as conflicting.

The question of race relations was early seen by the League to be a vital one in the interests of world peace.[7] The mandates were a collective measure to guard against racial abuses in the territories concerned.

In this context a significant development in South Africa, rebounding upon South West Africa, was the passing of the Colour Bar Act of 1926, which limited certain responsible and supervisory occupations to persons of European race. This raised not only the question of whether such discriminatory legislation was compatible with the mandate, but also the troubled issue of sovereignty, left ambiguous in the wording of Article 22: did the words 'as an integral portion of her own territory' confer on South Africa not only administrative but complete legislative freedom? Most of the Mandates Commission declared that the principles of the mandate must take precedence over Union legislation;[8] the Portuguese delegate claimed, as did South Africa herself, that special circumstances in the territory called for the modification of those principles.[9] South Africa finally accepted the Commission's conception, announcing that 'there is no statutory colour bar. . . . A certain colour bar [applying to certain types of employment] is . . . being observed in practice, but is certainly not a statutory enactment and is purely temporary, that is, until such a time as the native is sufficiently advanced to be able to undertake this responsible work'.[10] Despite this claim, however, an occupational colour bar has since been applied in South West Africa.

By this announcement the Union of South Africa admitted, albeit tacitly, that she did not believe the mandate authorized her to apply all her domestic policies to South West Africa.

Another of these policies which nevertheless was applied in the mandated territory was the system of native reserves and passes, which gave rise to further misgivings and controversy in the Mandates Commission and among interested observers. For administrative purposes South West Africa was divided into two zones, an arrangement inherited, with some slight modifications, from the German Administration; these are known as the

Police Zone and the Tribal Areas.* Lying to the south and including nearly three-quarters of the territory, the Police Zone is an area in which European laws are enforced; it contains, however, eighteen reserves into which non-Europeans are segregated. In its urban areas European residences and non-European locations are divided by 500-yard buffer strips. Residence by natives in these locations (about twenty–five in all) is by permit only; permits or passes are also required for all travel, and for employment or residence in the territory, except in the reserves.

The Tribal Areas are ruled indirectly through traditional chiefs under the supervisory authority of the Administrator of the territory; they are not settled by Europeans.

This system of segregation tends to keep the native inhabitants of the territory from any modernizing influence. It has been condemned as simply perpetuating the *status quo*;[11] other critics, however, have denounced the destruction of native organization by the invasion of white civilization.[12] The principle of the mandate idea concerned here was the effect the reserve and pass system might have on the civilizing mission enjoined on the mandatory power. The Mandates Commission found the system of reserves, of insulation from external ideas and influence, generally hard to reconcile with this spirit of the mandate;[13] South Africa claimed that conditions in the territory were such that the system was the appropriate means of promoting the material and moral welfare of the natives.

The Union was also responsible under the mandate for the social progress of the inhabitants of South West Africa. Educational policy is a useful guide to her objectives here. She has aimed at training the native populations gradually, so that they might in time be fit to administer their own affairs and to satisfy their own peculiar needs, always under the guidance of white officials—a policy she has described as one of benevolent tutorship.[14]

From the outset of the mandate the Union's educational policy has been condemned by the Commission, who felt that the Union's efforts had little effect on the native population.[15] They criticized the lack of government schools for the natives,

---

* See Map (page viii).

who were dependent for education on the efforts of various missionary societies, while the white population was directly provided for by the state. The missions were subsidized by the Administration, who claimed to be reluctant to disrupt their long-established civilizing influence, but the amounts allocated to white and native education were quite disproportionate: in the period 1925-32 twelve times as much was spent on the education of the white tenth of the population as on the native nine-tenths. The state thus spent on a white child 120 times the money allocated for each native. This the Union justified by saying that the white population's contribution to tax revenue was far greater; the bulk of taxes, however, were collected in indirect taxation on enterprises in the territory which were dependent on cheap native labour.

In any case the amount spent on education was too low: 1 per cent of the territory's revenue, lower than the proportion in any other 'B' or 'C' mandate. The Permanent Mandates Commission doubted whether this would enable backward races to stand alone, particularly in view of the fact that the existing education in the territory, far from advancing its inhabitants, was designed to perpetuate stagnant social structures at a deplorably low level. In contrast to inhabitants of such other mandates as Tanganyika, the natives of South West Africa received no training in administration or leadership, because white minority government was envisaged there. The fact that any government expenditure on native education was seen as a gesture of generosity rather than a duty could only perpetuate and accentuate inequality and division between the races, a result which was of no concern to the Union, who never envisaged a multiracial society for South West Africa and saw racial disparity as an inescapable phenomenon beyond fiscal control.

The Permanent Mandates Commission, however, was concerned only with the effect of the resulting policy on South Africa's international obligations, and it concluded that her educational policy in the territory fell short of what the mandate required.[16] In 1958 the Union's own Commission of Inquiry concluded that native education in the territory was inadequate.[17]

The Union was certainly, in the early days of the mandate, concerned to satisfy the Permanent Mandates Commission and to stand well in the opinion of the world, as a mandatory power; this may be seen by her handling of the Bondelzwarts and Rehoboth revolts, in 1922 and 1925 respectively. The former, a revolt of a Hottentot tribe subject since the time of the German administration to crippling penalization, was suppressed rigorously by the Union with bombs and aeroplanes. This and the consequent loss of life were condemned by the Mandates Commission as being out of keeping with the spirit of the mandate and more like the action of a colonial régime.[18] The unfavourable publicity which this incident received resulted in very different handling of the rising of the Rehoboth Bastards three years later. A tribe of mixed origin, they had enjoyed under the Germans a certain measure of internal autonomy under treaty rights which South Africa refused to restore, fearing to encourage more and similar claims. In 1924 a disagreement with the Administration over elections to the Rehoboths' Raad (legislative assembly) led to their petitioning the Permanent Mandates Commission and defying the Administration. Union forces entered their territory in April 1925 and they were forced to surrender. The Union, mindful of the adverse criticisms of the Bondelzwarts affray, handled this rising with special care to avoid casualties to the satisfaction of the League.[19] However, the affair pointed out a weakness in the mandate system, since decisions on constitutional issues were seen to be taken by the mandatory power rather than by the Mandates Commission, which refused to be involved in political controversy.

The exercise of South Africa's authority in and with regard to South West Africa constantly raised the question of sovereignty, already once referred to (see p. 9) The mandate authorized her to have full administrative and legislative power over the territory as an integral part of the Union. She tended to interpret this as virtual incorporation, but the Mandates Commission was sensitive and critical about any such suggestion. League organs, although they frequently discussed the location of sovereignty (carefully evaded at Versailles), avoided any authoritative statement; they did, however, agree that it did not reside in the mandatory power.[20] Consequently they objected to the Union's statement in the South West Africa Railways and Harbours Act of 1922 that these assets were conveyed 'in full dominion' to the Governor-General of South Africa, to be incorporated in the Union's system; the expression contravened Article 257 of the Treaty of Versailles and the mandate, and the Union had no right thus to annex or confiscate the railways and ports.[21] Requested to amend the Act, the Union procrastinated over a legal point, but finally complied eight years later.

A similar issue of sovereignty was raised by the 1926 agreement between the Union and Portugal about South West Africa's frontier with Angola; the preamble to this contained the words 'possess sovereignty' which the Mandates Commission denied. The Union in 1930 accepted the Council's resolutions on this,[22] which followed the argument of the Mandates Commission that the mandatory power could *exercise* the rights of sovereignty without actually *possessing* them. The Appellate Division of the South African Court considered in 1924, in *Rex v. Christian*, that the Union's exercise of sovereignty in South West Africa made possible the conviction for high treason of an inhabitant of the territory, based on the claim that he owed allegiance to George V. The Mandates Commission took exception to this view, nor had parallel cases in other mandated territories been so decided, a fact which reflected the differing conceptions of the legal relationship between mandatory and mandated territory.

One more related constitutional question was raised by the Union's proposal in 1924 to naturalize by Act of Parliament all the German inhabitants of South West Africa, who would, however, be given the chance to opt out. This arose from the Union's need for the co-operation of the white colonists if, as she wished, she was to grant some measure of self-government to this section of the territory's inhabitants. She already had, she said, adequate machinery for the government of native peoples, but was most reluctant to govern without representation those of European race. She therefore requested League permission for this move.[23]

The Mandates Commission, considering whether such action was within the rights of the mandatory power, felt it would assimilate the Germans with the inhabitants of the Union, destroying a vital distinction;[24] they felt that such collective and almost compulsory naturalization contradicted the principles of the mandate. Eventually, however, the Union's proposal was allowed with some reservations. It was followed in the territory by a measure of self-government (equivalent to that of a Province in the Union). The franchise was limited to the white inhabitants; the natives were stated by the Union to be as yet uncivilized and not fit for the franchise, although they would have some representation later. This assurance was not fulfilled. The native inhabitants were to continue to be administered from the Union, and not, South Africa assured the Mandates Commission, by the new South West Africa legislature;[25] this body did, however, have control of such matters as the education budget for the whole territory.

These policies, consciously planned and pursued by the Union Government, achieved a measure of political and economic integration between the two territories designed to rule out future separation. This close link was later to be used as an argument for incorporation.

As we have seen in this chapter, there was during this period latent conflict between the Union and the Permanent Mandates Commission—conflict which was later to develop into open antagonism.

3

SOUTH WEST AFRICA AND
UNION–GERMAN RELATIONS

THE dominating feature of South Africa's foreign policy between the wars was her desire to preserve her neutrality at all
costs and keep out of European quarrels. But South West
Africa's relationship with Germany made this policy difficult
to adhere to. South Africa from the start found her mandate
over South West Africa both an asset and a liability. Retention
of the territory was important to her for economic, strategic and
ethnological reasons; it entailed, however, certain risks and
sacrifices. Among the most complex of the problems involved
was that of the European population in South West Africa, and
the German element in this presented certain dangers and difficulties, actual and potential, to the Union.

South West Africa was unique among the mandated territories in retaining a large German element; elsewhere Germans
had been repatriated or expelled. In 1922, 10 per cent (19,432)
of the inhabitants were of European origin; of these rather under
half (7,855) were German. Doubts as to their legal status were
settled in 1924 by the South West Africa Naturalization of
Aliens Act (discussed in Chapter 2), allowed by the League with
some misgivings. This Act conferred British nationality on all
the German inhabitants of the territory, with an option of re-
nunciation within a specified period. It had been preceded in
1923 by an agreement with Germany over the status of her
nationals in the territory, whereby she recognized that the
future of South West Africa was now bound up with South
Africa, who for her part guaranteed to these Germans full

linguistic and cultural freedom. This concession by the weak Weimar Republic was, however, to be repudiated when a more nationalistic régime came to power in Germany.

In 1924 only 200 out of the 3,000 eligible adult Germans opted out of becoming British subjects. No such option was provided in the Union Nationality and Flags Act, in 1927, which conferred Union nationality on all British subjects in the territory; this of course included almost all the Germans in South West Africa. Such mass naturalization had been repeatedly stated by League organs to be contrary to the principles of the mandate,[1] and they opposed the scheme, as did the German Government and the South West Africa Germans themselves. Under a German law, however, it was possible for them, with the approval of their home State, to retain German nationality even though naturalized South Africans, and many did so. A special 'mandate citizenship' was also proposed by them, but not allowed by the Mandates Commission, despite its misgivings over the naturalization scheme, which were increased by the fact that anyone rejecting Union nationality was obliged either to leave the territory, all property and interests there, or to remain as an alien.

Most members of the League foresaw that this course of action would culminate, not in self-government of the territory as an independent unit, but in annexation pure and simple.[2] As far as South Africa was concerned, the settlement of the nationality issue was certainly the first step towards her eventual aim of incorporation.

The Union, however, did not secure the co-operation of the German inhabitants, as she had hoped, nor any willing allegiance. Indeed before long the Mandates Commission was petitioned by a prominent member of the community, who alleged discriminatory practices against Germans in the territory. German was not recognized as one of the official languages; German immigrants had to wait five times as long for the franchise as those of South African origin (on grounds of linguistic difficulty); the Germans feared their vote would be swamped by the repatriation in 1928 of 2,000 descendants of the Angolan Boers, who had fled British rule a century before; and they claimed that the Administrator used against them his right of nomination to the Legislative Assembly, to prevent the

Germans from playing their proper part in the administration of the territory.[3]

Relations with Germany were naturally very much affected by South Africa's position as the mandatory power for this former German colony. A European conflict in an African setting might undermine the whole foundation of European rule in Africa, on which the South African Government based all its policies. The Union's attitude towards Germany during this period was therefore a conciliatory one, beginning with the agreement with the Weimar Republic in 1923 and ending with outright support for German colonial claims—South West Africa always excepted. This territory, said the Union, was a special case; its links with the Union were too strong to make its return to Germany practicable. But she hoped by advocating the return of other former colonies to Germany to gain German support over South West Africa. Since, however, the other mandatory powers had no such notion, South Africa could offer Germany little but goodwill, which was coolly received.

The Nazi ideal of uniting the German *Volk* had obvious connotations for South West Africa. And the emergence of a rehabilitated, militarized Germany encouraged Germans there to hope for a return of the territory to German control. Events in Germany fostered the separatist movement and urged opposition to incorporation; Nazi organizations such as the *Hitlerjugend* were formed, and finally in 1935 the moderate *Deutsche Bund*, political party of most Germans in the territory, merged with the *Deutsche Front*, composed mainly of the fast-increasing non-naturalized immigrants from Germany. Conciliatory moves by the Administration, such as the establishment in 1932 of German as a third official language, easy naturalization and the promise of a Commission of Inquiry into economic conditions (which since the 1930 Depression caused the non-Germans to call for incorporation), all came too late: the links with Berlin were too strong. In 1933 and 1934 the Administrator had to adopt stringent measures against the Germans in order to maintain South African authority; Nazi organizations were banned, and their leaders expelled. Later legislation in 1937 barred any non-British subject from membership in a 'public body', which term included political parties. British subjects were forbidden allegiance to any foreign government or political organization.

It is, however, uncertain whether these measures stamped out Nazism in the territory or, more probably, merely drove it underground. Although they lowered tension locally, international relations were more than ever strained.

When Germany was admitted to the League of Nations in 1926, no objection had been raised in principle to her having colonies or mandates. This strengthened her case when she began to demand the return of her old colonies; she wanted no more, she said, than what she might thus legally claim. Hitler wanted an empire for reasons of political prestige; economically too it would provide a valuable market, and he demanded League discussions on colonial equality.

Although these demands met with some sympathy in Nationalist Party circles in the Union, South West Africans of Union origin were sufficiently alarmed by them and the German separatist movement in the territory to call in 1934 for the incorporation of South West Africa in the Union as a Fifth Province.[4] The Mandates Commission opposed this, guided by the view that the interests of the natives must be paramount.[5] In the event, the South African Government did not implement the proposal for union. A Committee of Inquiry instituted by the Union had failed to agree on a solution, though it found no objection to the Fifth Province idea; it had also made a number of economic proposals, found the natives to be well administered but in need of more advancement, and called for the abolition of the constitution.

It is against this background that South Africa's foreign policy in the 1930s must be seen, a policy of qualified isolation, of 'South Africa first'. The South West Africa mandate, however, involved the unwilling Union in the impending conflict: however much she reiterated that South Africa must be free to decide whether or not she would go to war, however much she desired peace at almost any price, almost no section of opinion in the Union was prepared to give up South West Africa. The Nationalist Party (then in opposition) in particular was much divided on the issue, and temporized for some time. But as Hitler's determination on world domination became apparent, as his colonial demands stepped up and he annexed one European territory after another and sent more Nazi agents to South West Africa, the danger to South Africa through the mandated territory became obvious to all, and the Union Government, urged by General Smuts, by a small parliamentary majority issued a declaration of war against Germany on 6 September 1939.

4

FROM THE LEAGUE
TO THE UNITED NATIONS

THE League of Nations and the United Nations Organization coexisted for six months, between October 1945 and April 1946. But the League took no steps during that period to transfer the remaining mandates; it dissolved intestate in this respect, and the new organization thus inherited a controversial problem as to their disposition. The South West Africa dispute today, and South Africa's case in particular, originates to a great extent in the uncertainties left by the League on its dissolution.

When, at its twenty-first and final session, the Assembly decided on the dissolution of the League, it recalled that Article 22 of the Covenant applied to certain territories placed under mandate, and recalled also the principle that the well-being and development of peoples not yet able to stand alone under the strenuous conditions of the modern world formed a sacred trust of civilization. It recognized that, on the termination of the League's existence, its functions with respect to the mandated territories would come to an end. It noted, however, that Chapters XI, XII and XIII of the Charter of the United Nations embodied principles corresponding to those declared in Article 22 of the Covenant of the League. Finally it took note of the expressed intention of the members of the League then administering territories under mandate to continue to administer them for the well-being and development of the peoples concerned, in accordance with the obligations concerned in the respective mandates, until other arrangements had been agreed upon between the United Nations and the respective mandatory powers.[1]*

The South African Government recognized, as did other mandatory powers, these continuing obligations until other agreements might be reached concerning the future status of the territory;[2] their representative added, however, that at the forthcoming session of the United Nations General Assembly in New York the Union would formulate its case for according South West Africa a status under which it would be internationally recognized as an integral part of the Union.

Such incorporation would have amounted to an end of the mandate, and for this, in the case of South West Africa, no procedure had been resolved before the dissolution of the League. Indeed, although it was widely accepted that mandates were temporary, no provision had been made in the League Covenant or in 'B' and 'C' mandate agreements for effecting their termination. It was not until 1930, in the context of the ending of the Iraq mandate in the 'A' class, that the Permanent Mandates Commission was asked to submit suggestions about the general conditions that must be fulfilled before a mandate could be brought to an end. Its report, adopted by the Council, stipulated the following conditions:

(a) it [the mandated territory] must have a settled government and administration capable of maintaining the regular operation of essential Government services;
(b) it must be capable of maintaining its territorial integrity and political independence;
(c) it must be able to maintain the public peace throughout the whole territory;
(d) it must have at its disposal adequate financial resources to provide regularly for Government requirements;
(e) it must possess law and a judicial organization which will afford equal and regular justice to all.[3]

The South African representative on the League Council reserved his Government's position on these conditions, feeling that they could only be applied to 'A' mandates.[4]

The League's winding-up resolution, the declarations by the mandatory powers and the Charter provisions, indicated,

* See Appendix III for some provisions of the UN Charter on trusteeship.

respectively, the desires of the League at its demise, the wishes of the mandatory powers, and the political intentions of the new United Nations with regard to the mandated territories. Nevertheless many vital issues were left unresolved, the most important being:

- (i) the survival or otherwise of the mandate system as a treaty in force after the demise of the League of Nations;
- (ii) whether or not the mandatory powers were obliged to conclude trusteeship agreements;
- (iii) the competence of the United Nations to exercise the supervisory functions of the defunct League of Nations.

In essence the South West Africa dispute has revolved round these three issues, and initially round the second cited here.

Articles 75, 77 and 80 of the United Nations Charter called for subsequent individual agreements placing mandates under the trusteeship system, and safeguarded all rights till then; this conservatory formula was not, however, to be interpreted as giving grounds for delay. Therefore the first session of the General Assembly, in its first part in February 1946, invited mandatory states to take practical steps, in concert with other states concerned, to submit trusteeship agreements for the approval of the General Assembly, preferably not later than during the second part of the first session. [5]

At the same session the Union's representative at the General Assembly formally reserved his Government's position on the future status of South West Africa, until it could conclude consultations with the African inhabitants regarding the incorporation of their territory into the Union. [6] However, he assured the United Nations that South Africa was fully conscious of her obligations under the Charter, which she would implement.

Draft trusteeship agreements for eight other mandated territories were presented at the second part of the first session of the General Assembly. South Africa, however, presented a 'memo on the administration of South West Africa and the wishes of its peoples as to the future status of the mandated territory presented by the Government of the Union of South Africa acting in the name of and on behalf of the people of

South West Africa',[7] This more or less repeated the reasons for incorporation which South Africa had advanced to the United Nations Conference on International Organization in 1945; the difference was that this time the reasons were presented on behalf of the inhabitants of the territory, rather than of the South African Government. They included an original uncertainty as to the suitability of the mandatory form of administration for South West Africa; the strategic relations between the mandated territory and the Union of South Africa; the composition and nationality of the European population of South West Africa, and the economic dependence of South West Africa on the Union of South Africa. Special emphasis was placed on the idea that South West Africa was physically incapable of affording a separate economic and administrative existence apart from the Union. The document submitted:

> the inference is inescapable that the backwardness of the inhabitants, the lack of material wealth and the geographical location of the country dictated administrative integration with the mandatory State and a separate administrative existence would be impossible of achievement.[8]

It was further argued that the incorporation sought was intended to give effect to the wishes of the peoples of South West Africa and hence that it was a logical application of the democratic principles of national self-determination envisaged by the Charter. The European population in South West Africa, it was claimed, expressed such a wish through a unanimous vote of the South West Africa Legislative Assembly; the wishes of the non-Europeans, it was reported, had been ascertained in an equally democratic but rather different form, through their traditional leaders. The referendum on incorporation showed 208,850 natives in favour with 38,520 against and 56,790 who could not be consulted.

General Smuts, South Africa's representative and an architect of the original mandates scheme, argued that the initiative for incorporation came from the people of the territory, whose spokesman merely he was, and who did not wish for a trusteeship agreement. Indeed, South West Africa was already so thoroughly integrated with the Union geographically, strategically and economically, that incorporation would only be a formal recognition of an actual and inevitable unity. Nor did he believe that the Union was obliged by the Charter to conclude a trusteeship agreement.

Political reasons were and are predominant in the Union's demand for incorporation. She distrusted the United Nations, largely because of its composition. It contained both backward and advanced nations, and many with no experience of African government. She disliked its egalitarianism and feared irresponsibility. Preferring the old League, mostly of nations of European stock, she realized that the entry into the dispute of the United Nations would have repercussions on native and coloured opinion in the Union.[9]

South Africa was also doubtful about the question of supervision of the mandate or trusteeship territory. The old Permanent Mandates Commission had been composed mainly of white colonial powers (see Chapter 2), who were likely to be friendly. Its members were chosen by the League as private individuals, and only then nominated to represent their governments. The Trusteeship Council which succeeded it was a principal organ of the United Nations, its members first and foremost representatives of their governments, and far more political in character. It was, moreover, empowered to make visits to the territories—with the consent of the administering power; and it made, to South Africa's annoyance, no differentiation between the different classes of mandate, although it expected variations in the trusteeship agreements to meet varying circumstances.

South Africa was suspicious of these changes in powers and composition. There was, moreover, an important change in outlook with the new organization. Emphasis in the mandates system had been on the welfare of the inhabitants of the territories; the trusteeship system has stressed the political self-determination of the peoples concerned. In both systems, however, the administering powers have had sole power of government, and the international organization has been merely supervisory and dependent for effect upon the power of public opinion.

The trusteeship question soon became a battleground for political warfare in the General Assembly of the United Nations. Knowing that the unpopularity of South Africa's case would prevent her from achieving much on political grounds, the Nationalist Party Opposition (soon to be in power) favoured basing the Union's case in the South West Africa dispute on legal, juristic grounds; they proposed incorporation on the grounds that:

(i) on the demise of the League, South Africa was not empowered to, and did not in fact, transfer its rights and powers in regard to South West Africa to the United Nations;

(ii) the Union was, and still is, *de jure* as well as *de facto* in possession of South West Africa;

(iii) the Union of South Africa has not by international agreement consented to surrender the rights so acquired, and has not surrendered such rights by signing the Charter of the United Nations;

(iv) the overwhelming majority of both the European and non-European population of South West Africa has expressed itself in favour of incorporation in the Union;

(v) in the circumstances the Union owes no responsibility whatsoever, as regards the administration of the territory, to the United Nations or to any other international organization or body.[10]

This is still the substance of the case of the Government of the Republic of South Africa today. In the early days of the dispute, however, General Smuts, regarding the Union's legal position as weak, based his claim on the 'factual position': 'the geographical position; identity of interests; the strategic position; ethnological relation between the natives of South West Africa and the Union; the suitability of the Union's administration for South West Africa; the existing measure of integration between the two countries and the expressed wish of both the native and European population'.[11] He did not contend that the Union's mandatory obligations ceased with the demise of the League.

South Africa's incorporation plan was opposed by all members of the United Nations except the United Kingdom. It met with most outspoken criticism from the Afro-Asian nations, led by the Indian delegate, who were supported by the Communist *bloc*. Most Western European nations, however, reserved their position, not condemning the South African Government outright. Only the United Kingdom delegate defended the proposal. This line-up in the international organization foreshadowed future groupings on the issue.

The Indian delegate's opposition to the plan was based on alleged discrimination against the natives of South West Africa, in such matters as segregation and inequalities in church and state, at work and in law. He believed the native population were not sufficiently advanced to have understood the consultations on incorporation or its implications, and he doubted the authenticity of the referendum.[12] His Afro-Asian supporters followed and repeated these accusations.[13] The members of the Communist *bloc* severally charged the South African Government with lack of good faith over the issue.[14] The most comprehensive condemnation, alleging violation of the principles of the Charter, was that of the Soviet delegate.[15] It is evident from these protests that the racial policy of the South African Government stood condemned before the United Nations and its members.

South African resentment of the United Nations' attitude was largely due to her realization that the issue was being used as a handle to indict her racial policies—and the colonial attitude in general—which she regarded as unjustifiable meddling in her domestic affairs. These criticisms the South African Government discounted as distorted, based on prejudice and ignorance; it particularly resented them as coming from India, a country whose social structure was highly discriminatory, and with whom too the Union had already an outstanding dispute over the South African Indian community. Europeans in the Union, who had for many years implicit faith in the League, distrusted the new organization, and opinion among them hardened in favour of incorporation of South West Africa; this, many felt, could well have been effected towards the end of the Second World War, a time when more nefarious annexations in other areas had been accepted by the United Nations as *faits accomplis*.

This consolidation of European opinion in the Union was hastened too by the protests of various minority groups within the country: non-European organizations, humanitarians, leaders of religious groups and socialist and Communist organizations, all of whom opposed incorporation because of South Africa's racialist policies. The equivalent organizations in South West Africa were equally strongly against the plan, especially nationalist groups who resented the denial of electoral rights to non-Europeans. Protests were also received by the United Nations from African and libertarian groups in Britain and the United States; and the Reverend Michael Scott, later to play a large part in South West African affairs, also protested to them. He alleged undue influence on the natives of the territory to gain their support for incorporation, and cited a number of instances; he claimed that the issues involved had not been properly explained to them, and that they disliked the Union's racial policies. The validity of the referendum was, moreover, widely questioned, on the grounds first that the wishes of officially recognized chiefs could not be a reliable guide to public opinion in a country of weakening tribal authority, and secondly that the figures obtained did not bear examination.[16] It was maintained, by the South African Institute of Race Relations, that illiterate natives in the territory were unlikely to have understood the implications of incorporation and probably thought it meant no more than the maintenance of the *status quo*.[17]

All these protests were naturally embarrassing to the South African Government, which declared that the issue was being made use of and inflated by left-wing subversionists, who found condemnation of racialism a useful pretext for organized political opposition to the Government. Certainly the stand of the Communist nations in the United Nations would support this view to some extent.

The almost unanimous agreement in the United Nations that South West Africa had international status made the Union's racial policies no longer a purely domestic issue as safeguarded in Article 2 (7) of the Charter. The Nationalist Opposition, however, so inexorably denied any United Nations concern with the mandate that they did not even want to submit information to the organization, as Smuts had proposed (he had declared that South Africa would administer the territory as an integral part of the Union, in the spirit of the mandate).[18]

Thus the South African Government, its good faith called in question by most of the United Nations, itself accused that organization of desecrating its lofty ideals. This spirit of mutual distrust was, therefore, hardly conducive to the settlement of the South West Africa question within a United Nations framework.

5

SOUTH WEST AFRICA AND THE UNITED NATIONS 1946-53

SINCE the end of the Second World War and the demise of the League of Nations in face of the establishment of the United Nations as the new international forum, the South West Africa debate has hinged on the legal issues involved, though these have, as was pointed out in Chapter 4, often served as a basis for political statements and action. In the period under discussion there was at first prolonged contention over the legality of the various issues involved; after a pronouncement had finally been made by an international legal organ, the arguments were dominated by the implications of this pronouncement.

The main point at issue was whether or not South Africa was legally obliged to conclude a trusteeship agreement for the territory, as provided in Articles 77 and 79 of the United Nations Charter of which she was a signatory (see Appendix III). In the first part of the first session of the General Assembly in 1946, South Africa had as we have seen reserved her position on the question of such an agreement; in the second part of the session she asked international recognition for South West Africa as an integral part of the Union. Various delegates, particularly the Communist *bloc*, condemned this contemplated annexation as violating the Charter. The General Assembly rejected this as a solution to the problem of South West Africa's future, noting, however, with satisfaction that, in bringing the matter before the United Nations for approval, South Africa recognized the interests and concern of the international organization. It was, however, political motivations, rather than the admission of a legal obligation, that led the Union thus to seek United Nations co-operation.

Nevertheless, South Africa bowed to United Nations opinion and did not proceed with the proposed annexation. She declined to submit a trusteeship agreement but would, she announced, maintain the *status quo*, administering the territory in the spirit of the mandate and submitting reports on her administration for the information of the United Nations.[1] These, however, would in no sense be an admission of United Nations jurisdiction, as they would be similar to the reports submitted for information purposes in respect of other non-self-governing territories in which the Trusteeship Council had no concern. Similarly, as there was no longer, since the demise of the League, an international organization whose supervisory function South Africa recognized, she put an end to the submission of petitions.[2] Since the so-called *status quo* thus excluded the international supervision formerly exercised by the League, the nature of the mandate would seem to be radically altered. The régime could only be described as *sui generis*.

Among the legal problems thus raised, the majority came under the following four heads: the assumption of the powers of the League of Nations by the United Nations; obligations under the United Nations Charter; the legal logic of the situation; and the will of the international community.

On the first of these questions, it was apparent that the new trusteeship system was more or less the same institution as the old mandates, with the same objectives; this the League, in its winding-up, had recognized (see Chapter 4, p. 20). It was a *de facto* substitute for the mandates system; the South African contention was that it was, however, not the successor to that system, since the League had made no such actual testamentary disposition. The Chinese and Indian delegates maintained that the United Nations *had* assumed the League's responsibilities in this sphere, and South Africa was therefore bound to make a trusteeship agreement with the organization.[3]

On the second question, it was provided in the United Nations Charter itself that the Charter should overrule all other international agreements; arguments on the permissive or compulsory nature of trusteeship were therefore based on the relevant Articles (75, 77, 79 and 80) of the Charter, to be found in

Appendix III. The 'compulsory' school of thought pointed to the words 'the trusteeship system shall apply . . .' in Article 77 (1); to the word 'voluntarily' in category 'c' of the same Article (implying obligation in category 'a', 'territories now held under mandate'), and attributed compulsion to Article 80 (2) which provided for delay or postponement (not failure) in concluding agreements. This view was held by the Afro-Asian and most Latin American countries, and the Communist *bloc*.[4] The 'permissives', comprising the USA, the white British Commonwealth nations and Western European countries, rested their argument on the consent of the states directly concerned, including the mandatory power, in the conclusion of any trusteeship agreement.[5] They drew authority from Article 75 (*e*) of the Charter, which spoke of individual agreements, as did Article 77 (1 and 2); from Article 79 which specifically stated that terms were to be agreed upon by states directly concerned; and from the conservatory clause in Article 80 (*i*), South Africa pointing out in particular the word 'may' in conjunction with the word 'agreements', implying a voluntary connotation.[6] The element of reason in both arguments points to yet another of the vague, contradictory expressions of intent which have confused this issue.

In the matter of the legal logic of the situation, it seemed that two inconsistencies would arise if South Africa could avoid the inclusion of South West Africa in the trusteeship system. First, it was argued by members of the group taking the 'compulsory' view that such contracting out could make the establishment of the whole trusteeship system impracticable.[7] However, the obligation to set up such a system, in Article 75 of the Charter, was laid not on the mandatory powers but on the United Nations. Secondly, the coexistence of two systems, if South Africa persisted in maintaining the mandate, was an obvious anomaly; there was therefore an attempt when the Charter was laid down to clarify the relevant Articles, making the trusteeship compulsory. But the permissive notion prevailed.[8]

Lastly, an issue which has naturally pervaded all discussion of the South West Africa problem, there was the question of the extent to which the will of the international community is binding on its members. World opinion was plainly in favour of trusteeship for South West Africa, and the smaller, relatively weak emergent states subscribed to the view that resolutions of the General Assembly of the United Nations were binding injunctions on its members.[9] Some larger and more powerful nations, such as France and the United States, felt that there was at least a moral obligation.[10]

The South African delegate, in response, denied that the spirit of the Charter enjoined that the legal rights of states under International Law should be held to be of no account, or that any state should abandon any trust under a mandate for another and a different trust, or that it should do so in defiance of the wishes of those primarily concerned: namely, the inhabitants of the territory held under trust. The General Assembly, he protested, was not the legislature of a world state, nor had its recommendations the force of law. He pointed out, moreover, that the Union had shown her respect for international opinion in complying with the United Nations' injunction against incorporation of South West Africa.[11]

Behind all these legal squabbles lay serious political differences. It was consistently obvious that the countries taking a permissive view of the trusteeship question were in the main the colonial and non-colonial powers; those who favoured compulsory trusteeship were the anti-colonialists. It was these political considerations which made for the uncompromising nature of the deadlock; there were, however, genuine legal points at issue which could only be resolved by an authoritative statement clarifying the position in law. It was first suggested in 1947 that the International Court of Justice be therefore asked for an interpretation of the Charter in this respect; two years of further argument were to elapse, however, before such a request was made.

An aspect of the South West Africa question that closely concerned the United Nations, and that has had considerable effect on the situation, is the proposed submission of annual reports. This was a feature of both the mandate and trusteeship systems, and was opposed by extremists on both sides, as compromising their position by implying acceptance of what both regarded as an unsatisfactory situation. Nevertheless South Africa did submit one such report in 1946, partly it seems as a compromise or gesture of goodwill, and firmly for information purposes and not for the scrutiny of the Trusteeship Council. This body did, however, proceed to examine it and to make sharply critical observations on the administration of the territory and its advancement, or lack of it, politically, economically, socially and educationally. In all these respects the Union's policy of racial segregation prevented, so the Council felt, the emancipation of the indigenous peoples.[12] South Africa, however, had implicit faith in that policy, which she justified as having the following objects:[13]

(*a*) to prevent race deterioration, to preserve race integrity and to give the different racial groups an opportunity to build up and develop their own race life;

(*b*) to protect each community against infiltration by the other;

(*c*) to prevent racial animosity which would inevitably arise if the life of the different races were inextricably mixed up;

(*d*) to prevent unemployment and the overcrowding of urban areas with all their attendant evils.

This explanation of the policy of segregation was that of the Nationalist Government which came to power in 1948 and which submitted no more reports. The Nationalists had always opposed the proposal of reports; they now repudiated General Smuts' original offer, emphasizing the voluntary nature of the report and the fact that it must create no precedent, particularly in view of the fact that the Trusteeship Council had exceeded its authority in dealing with the report.

The Nationalists, now the Government of South Africa, gave the following reasons for discontinuing reports:

(*a*) little understanding in the United Nations of the unique nature of the circumstances governing the relationship of South West Africa to the Union;

(*b*) little recognition of the assurances given that the territory would continue to be administered in the spirit of the mandate;

(*c*) that the information voluntarily furnished to the United Nations was being used to criticize, in an unwarranted manner, and to censure the Union Government in regard to its administration of the territory;

(*d*) that the Union Government would not agree, as certain delegations were contending, that its submission of reports was indicative of accountability to the United Nations for its administration of South West Africa.[14]

The Union Government now announced for the first time that the mandate was no longer in force, and hinted at a plan for closer association between the territory and the Union. This came in the South West African Affairs Amendment Act of 1949, which provided for representation of the territory in the Union Parliament. The representation and franchise were to be entirely European, though provision was made for one Senator nominated by the Governor-General for his knowledge of 'the reasonable wants and wishes of the coloured races of the territory'. The United Nations predictably condemned the measure for lack of franchise for the native 90 per cent of the population, as well as for its implications of incorporation and the legal aspects involved in view of South West Africa's international status.[15]

For its part, the South African Government was no less annoyed by the decision of the United Nations' Fourth Committee, in 1949, to grant an oral hearing to the Reverend Michael Scott, representing the indigenous population of South West Africa. This raised a legal problem in view of the fact that the old League had not admitted oral hearings. South Africa, originally included in the relevant sub-committee, withdrew her support; the remaining members (Egypt, Guatemala, the USA and Poland) were therefore joined by Columbia and Dominica, but the absence of South Africa and her sympathizers raised the presumption that the committee would not deal with the matter fairly.

Mr Scott brought with him eight documents conveying the views of Hereros, Hottentots, Namas and Berg Damaras;[16] on the basis of these he alleged that many of the Africans in the territory would have liked, and in fact had asked for, a United Nations Commission to be sent to investigate events and the opinions of the indigenous peoples on the spot, and from various incidents he inferred that the aims of trusteeship were not explained to the natives and the results of the referendum could not have presented an accurate picture of the situation. He appealed for United Nations help to right this.

The South African Government tried to discredit Scott, but this was not easy, for his criticisms and allegations were well documented, and most delegates seem to have been impressed by his integrity, zeal, moral conviction and dedication to the cause of equality of men. However, he undoubtedly, in interpreting political issues in religious terms, disregarded some of the legal and political issues involved in the dispute.

All these issues pointed to an impending deadlock at the United Nations over the status of South West Africa. The General Assembly was constrained to ask for a clarification of the legal issues involved in the dispute. Accordingly in 1949 the following questions were referred to the International Court of Justice for an Advisory Opinion:

> What is the international status of the territory of South West Africa and what are the international obligations of the Union of South Africa arising therefrom, in particular:
>
> (a) Does the Union of South Africa continue to have international obligations under the mandate for South West Africa and, if so, what are these obligations?
> (b) Are the provisions of Chapter XII of the Charter applicable and, if so, in what manner, to the territory of South West Africa?
> (c) Has the Union of South Africa the competence to modify the international status of the territory of South West Africa, or, in the event of a negative reply, where does competence rest to determine and modify the international status of the territory?[17]

The three legal issues on which opinion was divided and which the Court was asked to clarify were in effect: whether the mandate was a treaty in force; whether the Union was legally obliged to conclude an agreement; and whether the United Nations was legally competent to exercise the supervisory functions of the former League of Nations.

Four basic conclusions, which might be regarded as the fundamental legal conditions of the South West Africa régime, emerged from the Court's Opinion of 11 July 1950. The Court found unanimously that the South West Africa mandate was a treaty in force and that the competence to determine and modify the status of the territory rested with the Union of South Africa acting with the consent of the United Nations. By twelve votes to two, it further held the view that the supervisory functions of the League Council would have to be exercised by the General Assembly of the United Nations; but thirdly, that the degree of supervision to be exercised by the General Assembly should not exceed that which applied under the mandates system, and should conform as far as possible to the procedure followed in that respect by the League Council. Lastly, by eight votes to six, the Court was of the view that the provisions of Chapter XII of the Charter did not impose on the Union of South Africa a legal obligation to place South West Africa under the trusteeship system.[18]

The legal issues thus clarified, the United Nations' tasks were to persuade the South African Government to accept the Court's Opinion, to devise practical steps to conform with that Opinion and, in taking these steps to solve the problem, to obtain the co-operation of South Africa and her sympathizers.

The first of these aims proved impossible. An Advisory Opinion of the International Court of Justice has no binding character, and South Africa rejected this one. She regarded it as a misinterpretation of the law, and knew moreover that she need not be bound by it.

All the other United Nations delegations accepted the Advisory Opinion as a basis for further arrangements, but differed on the best procedure to adopt. The more moderate group (Argentina, Belgium, El Salvador, France, Iraq, the Netherlands, Norway, Peru, Sweden, Thailand, the United Kingdom, the USA and Venezuela) favoured negotiation and called for a committee to confer with South Africa on implementation of the Advisory Opinion; a second group (mainly Afro-Asian, with the remaining Latin Americans) thought that the machinery of implementation should be set up forthwith, without further negotiation. This division undermined both the authority and efficacy of the United Nations in dealing with the matter, and the Ad Hoc Committee finally set up was to perform both tasks: it was both a negotiating machinery and an interim supervisory body.

It cannot be said that the Advisory Opinion brought chances of settling the South West Africa dispute any nearer.

However, it did have some sort of calming effect, relaxing tension at the United Nations, and the Union Government did enter into limited negotiations on the basis of some of its findings.

The Ad Hoc Committee on South West Africa, established on 13 December 1950, was originally composed of the representatives of Denmark, Syria, Thailand, the USA and Uruguay. It was detailed to confer with the Union of South Africa concerning the measures necessary for implementing the Advisory Opinion. As an interim measure it was also authorized to examine petitions and reports on the administration of South West Africa, covering the period since the last report. Finally, it had to submit its own report to the next session of the General Assembly.

The Committee was handicapped from the start. Its terms of reference were limited to considering measures for implementing the Opinion—which South Africa had rejected. Its membership might have been more representative: it had no British Commonwealth member, the United Kingdom having refused to participate in handling the affairs of a fellow-member of the Commonwealth.[19] It was probably not really free to consider any final arrangement but trusteeship, and it was saddled with the task of supervising the mandate without access to information, South Africa having denied her accountability to the United Nations. Its two roles—negotiation and supervision—were difficult to combine: if, as seemed likely, it were to criticize the administration, it would spoil its chances of useful negotiation.

South Africa was, however, willing to enter into negotiations, with a definite reservation that the Advisory Opinion, lacking the status and authority of a judgment of the Court, was binding neither upon her nor upon the United Nations.[20] She now presented a proposal for an entirely new sort of supervision. Under her plan, she would resume her international obligations under the League mandate by negotiating a new agreement with the three remaining Principal Allied and Associated Powers of the First World War (France, the United Kingdom and the USA). She would administer South West Africa in the spirit of the mandate, but without petitions or annual reports. Although she denied that the United Nations was in any way the heir of the League, she would agree to its final confirmation of this agreement, and to the judicial supervision of the International Court of Justice in the event of non-compliance with its obligations; and indeed by thus submitting the plan she had, without admitting it, recognized the interests of the international community in the mandate.

The Ad Hoc Committee considered the plan unacceptable since it did not fully implement the Advisory Opinion. Ending annual reports and petitions was considered outside the terms of reference, and the proposed judicial supervision was inadequate, not conforming to the principle of international accountability, central to the idea of tutorship of backward peoples. Similarly, the plan did not include the United Nations or any of its agents, since the three Powers were to be Principals.

A counter-proposal by the Ad Hoc Committee called for the implementation of the Advisory Opinion by a procedure as near as possible to that of the League: a fifteen-member Committee to be appointed by the League, to include South Africa and with the supervisory functions of the League Council. This Committee would establish a special Commission on South West Africa, with the functions and responsibilities of the former Permanent Mandates Committee. South Africa, however, rejected this proposal: she would not compromise on the issues either of annual reports or of accountability to the United Nations.

The Ad Hoc Committee therefore had little to base its supervision on, and limited itself to the examination of communications to the Secretary-General on South West Africa, mostly protests from outside the territory. It made further attempts to negotiate in 1951, and reported agreement on the following:

(a) that a new instrument, replacing the mandate for South West Africa, should be concluded;

(b) that the new instrument should revive the 'Sacred Trust', with minor modifications necessitated by the changed circumstances but which would not in any way affect this principle;

(c) that, under certain conditions, the Government of the

Union of South Africa would make available information on its administration of South West Africa;

(d) that such information would be as full as that supplied by the Government of the Union of South Africa under the mandate system;

(e) that there should be some form of supervision of the Administration of South West Africa by the Union of South Africa.[21]

This apparent area of agreement gave rise to some optimism, but it was illusory: a superficial understanding had been achieved by temporizing omissions which glossed over the fact that basic differences remained on the vital questions of supervision, information and the second party to the agreement. Unless these could be amicably settled, the rest was meaningless. The Ad Hoc Committee insisted on United Nations supervision; South Africa would only be responsible to the Allies, and would conclude no agreement with the United Nations.

South Africa maintained moreover with some justice that United Nations supervision would extend South Africa's obligations under the mandate, as she would have to admit to the territory all missionaries of member states of the much larger and more comprehensive new organization. United Nations voting procedures, moreover, differed from those of the League, where decisions of substance must be made unanimously; in the United Nations a two-thirds majority sufficed.

At the United Nations General Assembly's seventh session in 1952 there was a moratorium on the South West Africa issue, since the Ad Hoc Committee had not produced proposals sufficiently precise and concrete for discussion; it was hoped thus to provide a political atmosphere conducive to further negotiations. At the eighth session next year, however, there was no more agreement: both sides simply reiterated their positions. The Ad Hoc Committee called for implementation of the Advisory Opinion (about which even the anti-colonialists had been divided, the Communist *bloc* taking a more rigid stance, while the Afro-Asians were anxious if possible to gain some South African co-operation). The Union continued to point out that the Opinion was not binding, maintaining too that the Court said nothing of a second party to the agreement.

38

South African opinion was hardening, as was that in the United Nations. No prospect of a solution was in sight, and the work of the Ad Hoc Committee on South West Africa was ignominiously brought to an end on 12 November 1953, giving place to another committee entitled the Committee on South West Africa.

6

SOUTH WEST AFRICA AND
THE UNITED NATIONS 1953–61

THE history of this second phase in the United Nations' effort to
reach understanding with South Africa is again a pattern of
predominantly political positions determining attitudes on the
legal issues involved. The Communist *bloc*, and generally the
Afro-Asian and Latin American nations, continued to press for
direct action to oblige South Africa to bring the territory under
United Nations trusteeship, and would allow of no compromise;
the Western European nations, the USA and the white British
Commonwealth, while supporting international concern with
South West Africa, were more accommodating in their conception of the ways in which this might be made effective.
South Africa throughout refused to allow that the territory was
the legitimate concern of the United Nations, and became
increasingly unwilling either to negotiate on the subject or to
find a compromise solution.

In November 1953 the General Assembly established the
Committee on South West Africa. In so doing it took note of
the International Court's Advisory Opinion of July 1950, and
reaffirmed that the South African Government still had international obligations in respect of the territory, and that the
supervisory functions of the old League of Nations were to be
exercised by the United Nations; this it felt the United Nations
owed to the inhabitants of the territory.

The seven-member Committee was requested to:

(*a*) examine, within the scope of the questionnaire adopted by the Permanent Mandates Commission of the League in 1926, such information and documentation as may be available in respect of the territory of South West Africa;

(b) examine, as far as possible in accordance with the procedure of the former mandates system, reports and petitions which may be submitted to the Committee or to the Secretary-General;

(c) transmit to the General Assembly a report concerning conditions in the territory taking into account, as far as possible, the scope of the reports of the Permanent Mandates Commission of the League of Nations;

(d) prepare for the consideration of the General Assembly a procedure for the examination of reports and petitions which should conform as far as possible to the procedure followed in that respect by the Assembly, the Council and the Permanent Mandates Commission of the League of Nations.[1]

It is noteworthy that this Committee, unlike its unsuccessful predecessor the Ad Hoc Committee on South West Africa, was specifically restricted by its terms of reference to measures necessary to implement the 1950 Advisory Opinion—which South Africa had rejected—and scarcely had room to explore other possible solutions.

The members of the Committee were Brazil, Mexico, Norway, Pakistan, Syria, Thailand and Uruguay. No member either of the Communist *bloc* or of the white British Commonwealth was on the committee, an indication of the suspicion by most delegations of the political motivations of the great power-*blocs* which had hindered objectivity in earlier negotiations. Representation was again by governments, rather than by individual experts as in the League's system, even though this Committee was to carry out the functions of the old Permanent Mandates Commission in the spirit of the mandate.

Still unresolved remained all the major differences which had hampered the work of the Ad Hoc Committee: the problem of oral hearing of petitioners, the question of South Africa's accountability to the United Nations and the General Assembly's insistence on trusteeship as the only acceptable future (apart from independence) for the territory. The new committee thus inherited all the problems of the old and was in almost every way analogous to it, with almost identical terms of reference and, eventually, all the same members. It had more-over to work in a political atmosphere of even more suspicion. It did so for eight thankless years, during which time it tried to perform such tasks as were assigned to it by the General Assembly.

One of the Committee's specific tasks was to draft rules for the examination of reports and petitions concerning South West Africa. One of these rules, special rule F, provided that questions in this connexion should be regarded as 'important questions' requiring a two-thirds majority for their decision; since this differed from the unanimity rule of the old League (whose procedure was to be followed as far as possible) it was proposed, should South Africa object to the rule, to ask the International Court for another Advisory Opinion on the matter.

Not surprisingly, South Africa did object: the proposed rule, by depriving her of the power of veto she had under the League's unanimity rule, would be increasing the degree of supervision over the territory. In this she was supported by France and Britain; fifteen more countries abstained from voting on the issue, some (the Communist *bloc*, Bolivia and Uruguay) because they favoured more direct political action, some (Australia, Belgium and New Zealand) because they thought the voting procedure rather stringent. Thus the emergent countries had not, in their efforts to deal with South West Africa, the support of either power-*bloc*, or the co-operation of South Africa.

After prolonged argument and virtual deadlock over this question of voting, it was agreed to ask the International Court for an Advisory Opinion:

(*a*) Is the following rule on the voting procedure to be followed by the General Assembly a correct interpretation of the Advisory Opinion of the International Court of 11th July 1950:

'Decisions of the General Assembly on questions relating to reports and petitions concerning the territory of South West Africa shall be regarded as important questions within the meaning of Article 18, Paragraph 2, of the Charter of the United Nations'?

(*b*) If this interpretation of the Advisory Opinion of the Court

is not correct, what voting procedure should be followed by
the General Assembly in taking decisions on questions relating to reports and petitions concerning the territory of
South West Africa?[2]

The pattern of voting on this issue was much as usual: the Communist *bloc*, favouring United Nations action without juridical
delay, opposed asking for an Opinion, which had been an
Afro-Asian–Latin American initiative, though many of these
emergent countries abstained. The Western *bloc* divided: some
abstained, some supported the resolution.

The International Court had thus been asked to interpret
a passage laying down first, that United Nations supervision
should not exceed that of the mandate; and secondly, that it
should conform as far as possible with League procedure. In
ascertaining what League practice had been, it became apparent
that mandatory powers had had a virtual veto in matters concerning their mandate, since they always attended relevant
meetings and voted there. There had in fact never been a
negative vote.

It would seem therefore that rule F, since it thus entailed a
greater degree of supervision than the League's, failed to conform with the 1950 Advisory Opinion. However, all fifteen
Judges of the International Court were of the opinion that the
rule was a correct interpretation of the Advisory Opinion. This
was because, they said, the term 'degree of supervision' referred
there to substantive matters rather than procedure. On con-
formity 'as far as possible' with League procedure, the Court
could not envisage how one system could be substituted for the
other without constitutional amendment, as the voting systems
were characteristic of different organizations. It held:

The authority of the General Assembly to exercise supervision
over South West Africa as a mandated territory is based on the
Charter (Article 10). While in exercising that supervision the
General Assembly should not deviate from the mandate, its
authority to take decisions in order to effect such supervision is
derived from its own constitution. . . . It would be legally impossible for the General Assembly, on the one hand, to rely on the
Charter in receiving and examining reports and petitions concerning South West Africa, and on the other hand, to reach
decisions relating to these reports and petitions in accordance

with a voting system entirely alien to that prescribed by the Charter.[3]

The General Assembly accepted this Advisory Opinion, in December 1955, by fifty-four votes to none, with four abstentions.[4] South Africa declared herself unaffected by it: since she denied all United Nations supervision, she cared little what procedure might be proposed. This stand, however, risked alienating her sympathizers; this issue was purely a legal one, so the General Assembly's political hostility to her was irrelevant here. At any rate, the Advisory Opinion enabled the United Nations to proceed with its attempt at supervision of the administration of the mandate, without South African co-operation.

The next legal issue to be clarified, so that the Committee on South West Africa might fulfil its task, was the admissibility of oral hearings. This had been an exasperating point of difference between the Government of South Africa and the Ad Hoc Committee.

Although the right of petition had been introduced into the mandate system in 1923, the Permanent Mandates Commission had never granted oral hearings. There had in fact been a Council resolution in 1927 which saw no need for such a modification of procedure;[5] the Commission had felt that in some cases it might be desirable, but all the mandatory powers had opposed it as making the Permanent Mandates Commission into a court of law, and having an unconstructive, disruptive effect on the territories.[6] However, the Council left a loophole by permitting 'such exceptional procedure as might seem appropriate and necessary in ... particular circumstances'.[7] Moreover, the decision against oral hearings was based on the assumption of the mandatory powers' continuing co-operation.

After the demise of the League it became increasingly clear that this co-operation was not to be forthcoming from South Africa. In 1949 she notified the Secretary-General of the United Nations that she would submit no more reports on South West Africa, that she would not submit petitions from the inhabitants of the territory or otherwise provide information to the United Nations.

This was a serious handicap to the Committee which,

although it was able to receive petitions sent to the Secretary-General (deemed to be validly received if also submitted to the Government of South Africa but not forwarded), lacked both South Africa's comment on petitions and the supplementary information only she could supply.

The Committee also now proposed, in its attempts to maintain international supervision of the territory, to allow oral hearings, and asked the General Assembly to determine whether these were admissible.[8] Before the International Court could be asked for an Advisory Opinion, the Fourth Committee had again granted a hearing to the Reverend Michael Scott; this move was opposed at this stage not only by the Western European countries but by many of the emergent nations, who expressed their misgivings over the wisdom of granting oral hearings in defiance of the objections that were being raised against the procedure on legal grounds.

The International Court was now asked:

> Is it inconsistent with the Advisory Opinion of the International Court of Justice of 11th July 1950, for the Committee on South West Africa established by the General Assembly resolution 749a (VIII) of 28th November 1953, to grant oral hearings to petitioners on matters relating to the territory of South West Africa?[9]

By eight votes to five, the International Court found that oral hearings would not be inconsistent with its 1950 Advisory Opinion; but the General Assembly must be satisfied that such a course was necessary for the effective international supervision of South West Africa. The Court justified oral hearings partly on the grounds of South Africa's refusal of co-operation to implement the Advisory Opinion of 1950, partly by the idea that the General Assembly, as successor to the League Council, was empowered to do all that the Council could, including what the Council had had no occasion to do. Oral hearings, it was thought, would give the Committee a better chance to judge of the merits of petitions, and hence not add to the burdens of the mandatory power.[10]

Although the admission of oral hearings would seem, despite the 1950 Advisory Opinion, to add to the degree of supervision of the mandate, these new powers were granted on the grounds of the two other main instruments of supervision (annual reports and written petitions) having been greatly reduced by the attitude of the South African Government. And this Advisory Opinion contained a number of limitations and safeguards to these powers. First, only the General Assembly could authorize the procedure for oral hearing of petitioners. Secondly, only those who had already submitted written petitions were eligible for oral hearing. Thirdly, the procedure was to be resorted to only in exceptional circumstances, in the absence of any of the regular means of supervision. Lastly, oral hearings were only justified on the ground of South Africa's abuse of rights.

Although ten other states abstained from voting on the adoption of this Opinion, only the United Kingdom opposed it, arguing that too much of the International Court's reasoning was based on hypothesis and outside its terms of reference.[11]

Although the Advisory Opinion did not much advance the solution of the South West Africa question—and indeed probably further estranged the parties to the dispute—the backing of such an authoritative ruling helped the Committee on South West Africa to proceed with its supervisory work. The Fourth Committee for its part proceeded in 1958 to hear the oral testimony of the Reverend Michael Scott and Mr Mburumba Kerina, a South West African native leader; South Africa refused to participate and the United Kingdom agreed, maintaining that the appearance of private individuals before a Committee of delegates of states was improper.[12]

These petitioners made a series of demands, some of them inconsistent. They were followed from 1959 to 1961 by a large number of native oral witnesses, many of whom had been obliged to leave the territory by clandestine means. They included Mr Jariretundu Kozunguire, representing the Herero tribe; Mr Sam Nujoma, co-founder of the Ovambo People's Organization and founder and first President of the South West Africa Peoples' Organization (SWAPO); Mr Vat ka Kaukuetu, Vice-President of the South West Africa National Union (SWANU); the Reverend Markus Kooper; Mr Jacob Kuhaugua, co-founder of the Ovambo People's Organization; Mr van Ismael Fortune; Mr Moses Goroeb; Mr Charles Kauraisa, an educationist and former teacher; Mr Zedekia Ngavirue, journalist and Adviser to the SWANU National Executive, and Mr Oliver Tambo, Deputy President-General of the African National Congress of South Africa. In general, the petitioners advocated the removal of the South African Government from authority over the territory's administration, the establishment of United Nations trusteeship over the territory preparatory to the grant of self-government and independence, United Nations intervention by establishing a Commission or similar body within the territory and the provision of technical and other assistance for the territory by the Specialized Agencies and Children's Fund of the United Nations.[13]

A rather different oral hearing, with sensational results, was centred on the evidence of three young Americans who, granted the opportunity to visit the territory to study wild life, surreptitiously recorded evidence of maladministration against the South African Government, who have since refused to grant permission for other scholars to enter the territory for any academic purpose.

The Fourth Committee, at the risk of still further estranging South Africa, insisted on these oral hearings although there were other means of supervision: the prospects of receiving written petitions from the territory were good, and many petitions were in fact received and examined. The only merit of the oral system was the opportunity it gave delegates to assess petitioners for themselves and thus evaluate their evidence. The South African Government, in particular the Prime Minister, Dr Verwoerd, certainly made every attempt to discredit them, labelling them subversive agitators. They were obliged to remain in exile, a fact which inevitably has to some extent deprived them of authentic knowledge of current conditions in the territory, and has tended to mean that the home front lacked leadership. Moreover, they have sometimes claimed undue international recognition, declaring themselves a government-in-exile.

Meanwhile, the Committee on South West Africa had embarked on its task of studying conditions in the territory with a view to preparing a report for the General Assembly. Meeting once again with no co-operation from the South African Government, but rather with reiterated denials of international commitment, and unwillingness to negotiate, the Committee had to draw on whatever information it could get. This came largely from published sources of United Nations Specialized Agencies and from official documentation published by the South African Government, and on the basis of such information the Committee issued its first annual report in June 1954.

About half of this report was a factual description of conditions in South West Africa, the rest a restatement of the course of the dispute and the status of the territory. It referred to the lack of participation by natives in the judicial organization of the territory, the existence of corporal punishment, forced residence, an undeveloped penal system and racially discriminatory legislation in the territory. It noted with grave concern the disparity between the expenditure on European and non-European education, and condemned the extremely low economic level of the native inhabitants, restrictions on their movement, their unsatisfactory labour conditions and legislation which, in effect, imposed forced labour on non-Europeans for the benefit of the Europeans. The report concluded:

> After 35 years of administration under the mandates system, the native inhabitants are still not participating in the political development of the territory, . . . their participation in the economic development is restricted to that of labourers, and . . . the social and educational services for their benefit are far from satisfactory.[14]

Between 1954 and its dissolution in 1961 the Committee on South West Africa submitted eight annual reports,[15] all without the co-operation of the South African Government. Generally they showed particular concern for and anxiety over the fate of the non-white inhabitants of the territory; they were for the most part critical of South Africa's administration. For instance, the Committee expressed deep concern over the disparity in land allocations: 45 per cent allotted to the Europeans who were less than 12 per cent of the population, 20 per cent to the non-white 88 per cent. Several reports claimed that the territory was being administered almost exclusively in favour of European inhabitants at the expense of the native population, in contravention both of the spirit of the mandate and the

Declaration of Human Rights. In 1957 the Committee made recommendations calling for:

(a) the progressive transfer of responsibility to representative, executive and legislative institutions proper to the territory;

(b) the revision of existing policies and practices of native administration in accordance with the spirit of the mandates system;

(c) the extension to all the inhabitants of representation in the existing territorial legislature;

(d) the basing of public employment on qualification other than race and the progressive training of non-Europeans for higher posts in the Administration;

(e) the review and revision of the land settlement policy;

(f) the discontinuance of residential restrictions based on a policy of racial separation, or *apartheid*, and the repeal of laws of the territory having racially discriminatory restrictions;

(g) the immediate elimination from the law and practice of the territory of the existing discriminatory restrictions upon freedom of movement;

(h) the elimination of racial discrimination from the educational system and the establishment of a programme for the progressive unification of the system;

(i) the exploration of ways and means of securing technical and financial assistance from the United Nations, and its specialized agencies, for the conservation and development of the territory's natural resources for the benefit of all sections of the population.[16]

Relations with South Africa worsened as the Committee's reports grew increasingly exasperated and the South African attitude hardened, persuasion becoming less and less effective. South West Africa was being constantly more closely bound to the Union, constitutionally and administratively. The Native Affairs Administration Act of 1954 transferred control of these matters to the Union's Minister of Native Affairs; native reserves were also administered from there. And South Africa's determination against international control at last resulted in the withdrawal in 1955 of her offer to negotiate an agreement with the Allies of the First World War.

South African co-operation and goodwill were plainly

essential for the supervision of the mandate. The United Nations could not proceed unilaterally, and new conciliatory measures were experimented with in order to break the impasse.

In 1957 the membership of the Committee on South West Africa was increased from seven to nine, and a system of rotation introduced to allow the maximum number of members (and shades of politics) to take a part in the Committee's work. The Committee was then asked to study what legal action was possible to ensure that South Africa fulfilled her mandatory obligations. The Committee recommended:

(i) that States, severally and collectively, could bring their disputes with the mandatory power, relating to the mandate, for compulsory jurisdiction of the International Court in accordance with Article 7 of the mandate;*
(ii) that organs of the United Nations could request the Advisory Opinion of the International Court not only on certain aspects of the supervisory procedure as requested in the 1955 and 1956 Opinions, but also on specific acts of the mandatory power such as the modification of the status of the territory in a manner or to a degree considered to be incompatible with the mandate.[17]

Pending such legal action, various members of the Committee put forward suggestions; the most comprehensive proposal was that of the Philippines, giving the following alternatives: holding a plebiscite, the application of Article 14 of the Charter for the peaceful settlement of the problem, the imposition of sanctions as provided for in the Charter, negotiations between the remaining Principal Allied and Associated Powers and the South African Government, a visit to the territory by an impartial observer or by representatives of Specialized Agencies of the United Nations to study conditions there, and the provision of technical and financial assistance to the territory.[18] But none of

---

* From this springs the Ethiopian and Liberian action against South Africa in the International Court in 1965. However, doubts were expressed as to which categories of States might have the right to take such action; hence, later, the choice of Ethiopia and Liberia, members of the original League, as plaintiffs.

these suggestions could then be translated into practical policy.

The only proposal which proved to be of practical significance as a conciliatory move was that which resulted in the establishment in October 1957 of the Good Offices Committee, to find a 'basis for an agreement which would continue to accord to the territory of South West Africa an international significance'.[19] The significance of this new move is in the Committee's composition and wide terms of reference: its members were the United States, the United Kingdom and Brazil, and its terms of reference said nothing of supervision and did not preclude other arrangements besides a trusteeship agreement. Because of this, and because it included two of the three remaining Principal Allied and Associated Powers of the First World War, the South African Government consented to enter into negotiations with it.

The Soviet *bloc* had opposed the creation of the new Committee, suspecting it of being a manœuvre of the Western powers to remove the issue from the United Nations; nor were the Afro-Asian countries enthusiastic. But it did result in a lessening of tension, in the return of South Africa to the Fourth Committee which she had boycotted because of its discussion of her *apartheid* policy, and in a pause in the overtures of the Committee on South West Africa to the South African Government. Cautious optimism was felt at the United Nations.

At its preliminary meetings in May 1958 the Good Offices Committee decided, as a guiding principle, that the supervisory authority of the United Nations must be clearly recognized as a minimum condition of any compromise with the South African Government.[20] Two alternative proposals were drawn up for the consideration of the South African Government: the establishment, with suitable adaptations to a United Nations context, of a system analogous to that under the League; or the placing of the territory under the International Trusteeship System. The latter South Africa once more summarily rejected, as by the 1950 Advisory Opinion she was legally free to do; and it soon became plain that neither side would yield on the vital issue of accountability to the United Nations.

However, there were four hopeful signs. These were: South Africa's acceptance of 'international character' for the territory, her offer to make available information on South West

Africa, an invitation to the Committee to visit the Union and the territory, and South Africa's willingness to consider a partition scheme. Unfortunately none of these promising indications was to lead to much advance. The first ended only in a revival of South Africa's former offer to negotiate with the remaining Allies of the First World War, an offer already repeatedly refused by the General Assembly in the light of the 1950 Advisory Opinion and now only noted by the Committee without comment. Nor was the offer of information acceptable, since it was made clear that it was not a formal report and in no way changed South Africa's juridical position. Two members of the Committee did actually visit the territory, but South Africa announced that her attitude was in no way changed because of this. And on partition no more progress was made; when the Good Offices Committee urged consideration of the idea, no member of the United Nations spoke in its favour. It was assumed—possibly wrongly—that South Africa would annex the southern and richer part of the territory, administering the north (where most of the native population lived) under a trusteeship agreement. South West Africa would then cease to be a multiracial State; discussions on her future would thus be insulated from the issue of racialism, and the United Nations would (most members felt) be endorsing *apartheid*, besides going back on earlier resolutions on the territory's integrity. Nevertheless, partition need not have been on such lines.

Thus the discussions of 1959 were doomed to be fruitless, since no basis for agreement existed. In view of this, the Committee on South West Africa began to take a tougher line, calling in 1959 for the alteration of the administration without delay, and accusing South Africa of violating both the mandate and the United Nations Charter on the following counts:

(a) Application of *apartheid* policy and of related legislative and administrative measures which established the rights and duties of various sections of the population on the basis of their colour, race and tribal origin.

(b) Failure to promote and protect the rights and interests of the indigenous population and of the territory as a whole.

(c) Denial to the native population of all basic human rights and fundamental freedoms.

(d) Continued failure to recognize and to submit to the supervisory authority of the United Nations over the administration of the mandated territory.

(e) General exercise of powers of administration and legislation in a manner inconsistent with the international status of the territory.[21]

The United Nations was urgently called to consider the implementation of the Committee's recommendations, which in 1961 were:

(a) the immediate institution of a United Nations presence in South West Africa;

(b) removal of the South African Administration from the territory of South West Africa, with effective and simultaneous transfer of power to the United Nations or to the indigenous inhabitants, either through the Committee on South West Africa or through a United Nations Special Committee of Assistance to South West Africa;

(c) training and organization of an indigenous police by the United Nations, withdrawal of firearms from all Europeans, prohibition of the possession of arms by all civilians, withdrawal of South African military forces, abolition of all organized immigration of Europeans, especially South Africans, to the mandated territory;

(d) attainment of independence by South West Africa through a constitutional convention, the election of the representatives of the people on the basis of universal adult suffrage and the establishment of an independent Government with the assistance of the Committee on South West Africa or the United Nations Special Committee of Assistance to South West Africa;

(e) schemes leading the indigenous inhabitants to the attainment of internal self-government and eventual independence, such as: an education system, a popular referendum, an economic organization, an agrarian organization and reform, and technical and economic assistance by the United Nations and its Specialized Agencies.[22]

Such action would obviously entail the surrender by South Africa of all her rights in the territory, when in fact she was clearly not prepared even to negotiate. Why therefore did the Committee put forward such extreme proposals? The cause seems partly to have been frustration after years of fruitless work, partly a desire to put South Africa in the wrong before world opinion. At all events the report was backed up by the United Nations; the Fourth Committee endorsed it by a high majority, as it had earlier and similar reports. Yearly the South African Government had been invited by the General Assembly to negotiate a settlement; yearly too it had been urged to conclude a trusteeship agreement, and it seems unlikely that the Committee on South West Africa was expected to negotiate towards any other settlement.

When it became obvious that the Union would not accept these yearly invitations, they were dropped from General Assembly resolutions. These resolutions became increasingly exasperated and censorious, beginning with an expression of 'deep concern' over conditions in the territory, declaring later that the administration was contrary to the mandate and the Charter, and finally considering the situation in South West Africa as a serious threat to international peace and security.[23]

All this virile condemnation must, however, be seen in its political context. The membership of the Committee on South West Africa was heavily anti-colonial; the authenticity of its conclusions must be open to doubt, particularly in the absence of reliable evidence on which to base its reports.

This second phase of negotiations between the United Nations and the Union of South Africa ended once more without prospects of a solution to the South West Africa question. If anything, the situation had worsened: South Africa was more determined than ever not to let the territory come under the jurisdiction of a United Nations increasingly hostile to her racial policy. The United Nations for its part was uncompromisingly rigid in its insistence on the terms of the 1950 Advisory Opinion, and specifically on United Nations control; this, it was clear, South Africa would never, short of compulsive measures, accept. Plainly a new approach was needed, particularly in view of the decolonization of the rest of Africa while the *status quo* persisted in South West Africa.

7

A NEW ERA: FROM 1960

THE growth of African nationalism and its increasingly free expression and scope have naturally affected South West Africa in a number of ways. First among these was the widespread change-over, after 1960, from colonial régimes to independence, which not only affected the climate of African opinion but radically changed the balance of power in the United Nations. Of the seventeen new members admitted in 1960, sixteen were newly independent African states. The African group thus swelled from nine to twenty-five (excluding South Africa), and the Afro-Asian group now comprised forty-six out of the United Nations' ninety-nine members. With the twenty-one Latin American states, the anti-colonialists commanded about two-thirds of the votes in the General Assembly; their position had become an extremely strong one. South Africa was less than ever likely to be willing to allow any control to such a hostile body. The distinction between South West Africa and the ordinary colonial régime was becoming increasingly blurred, and the problems of the territory were a convenient platform for anti-colonial statements. These had the active support of the Communist *bloc*, and the Western powers, hitherto reluctant to condemn South Africa even when they withheld actual support, were anxious now not to alienate the emergent states and drive them towards the Communist countries. South Africa thus found herself more isolated than ever before.

African nationalism was manifested in the territory itself in the emergence for the first time of non-European political organizations. Two were launched in 1959: the Ovambo People's Organization, which a year later had become a nation-

wide party under the name the South West Africa Peoples'
Organization (SWAPO), and the South West Africa National
Union (SWANU). Both favoured the ending of racial discrimina-
tion in the territory and removal of South African control, prior
to the grant of independence; both have been in touch with
African nationalist movements in South Africa and other
African states.[1]

These parties, and other elements both in and outside the
territory, have called for United Nations presence in South
West Africa, not only in general but specifically and immediately in the form of the Specialized Agencies of the organization. A four-year standing drought was in 1960 the occasion of
the General Assembly inviting the Specialized Agencies and the
Children's Fund to undertake urgent programmes to assist the
indigenous population.[2] The South African Government, however, refused co-operation, so this plan could not be put into
effect. But it does seem likely that the call of the Odendaal
Commission of Inquiry for much-accelerated development of
the natives may be the result of South Africa's awareness of
United Nations determination.

Probably the most far-reaching manifestation of African
nationalism was the request of the second conference of Independent African States, at Addis Ababa in 1960, that the
Governments of Ethiopia and Liberia institute contentions
proceeding against the South African Government on the
ground of violation of her obligations under the mandate.[3]
Consequently these two governments (chosen as being the only
African states who were members of the League and so had the
right thus to arraign South Africa) in November 1960 asked the
International Court to adjudge and declare that, as the mandatory power for South West Africa, South Africa has violated
her obligations under the mandate on the grounds of:

(a) Introduction of the practice of *apartheid* into the territory
of South West Africa.
(b) Adoption and application of legislative and administrative
regulations and official actions which suppress the rights
and liberties of inhabitants of the territory essential to their
orderly evolution toward self-government.
(c) Failure to render to the General Assembly of the United
Nations annual reports containing information with regard

to the territory to indicate the measures it has taken to carry out its obligations under the mandate; and failure to transmit to the General Assembly petitions addressed to it from the territory's inhabitants.

(d) Exercise of powers of administration and legislation over the territory that are inconsistent with its international status.

(e) Certain specific complaints such as:

    (i) Limiting franchise to persons of European descent.

    (ii) Depriving African children of adequate educational facilities.

    (iii) Requiring Africans to possess passes to travel beyond the confines of particular locations.

    (iv) Prohibiting Africans from membership of political parties and Trade Unions.

    (v) Segregating the inhabitants of the territory in residential areas according to race, colour, national and tribal origin.

    (vi) Excluding non-Europeans from engaging in occupations such as the following: dealing in unwrought precious metals; prospecting for precious and base minerals; officer in the Police Force; manager, assistant manager, sectional or underground manager, mine overseer, shift boss, ganger, engineer, surveyor, supervisor of boilers and engines in mines owned by persons of 'European' descent.

    (vii) Favouring 'Europeans' to the detriment of 'non-Europeans' in allocation of territorial land.

    (viii) Subjecting inhabitants of the territory to forcible deportation upon unreviewable orders of the Administrator of the territory.[4]

This move by the African states, stemming from the failure of negotiations between the United Nations and South Africa, represents a desperate effort to maintain the rights of the United Nations and its members in the mandate. It is of interest as an indication of unanimous agreement on the issue amongst African nationalists, and it is evidence of African determination to erase colonialism from the continent.

South Africa contended that the Court had no jurisdiction in the case. She submitted four preliminary objections: that the mandate was not, since the dissolution of the League, a treaty in force within the meaning of Article 37 of the Statute of the

Court; that there could, since that dissolution, no longer be 'another member of the League'; that the question before the Court was not a dispute as envisaged in Article 7 of the mandate; and finally that if such a dispute existed, it was not one which could not be settled by negotiation with the applicants and there had been no such negotiations with a view to settlement.[5] The Court, however, by a narrow majority (eight votes to seven) found against these objections and ruled that it was competent to exercise jurisdiction.[6] It was in fact being asked to repeat its 1950 Advisory Opinion in a binding form; it would be a major setback for the United Nations in general and the anti-colonialists in particular if that Opinion were to be reversed. If it is upheld, the Court would thereby declare that the mandate has been violated, and it could be legally revoked.

It was on the grounds that this issue was *sub judice*, and that no action should be taken that was likely to hinder, embarrass or prevent the Court's judicial function, that South Africa refused to co-operate when the Committee on South West Africa in 1961 tried to visit the territory, at the General Assembly's request. She refused visas to the members of the Committee, who were moreover unable to count on any help from the United Kingdom and Portugal, whose colonial territories adjoined South West Africa. (The West European powers had abstained from the General Assembly resolution calling for the visit.) Portugal refused visas; the United Kingdom granted them for Bechuanaland so that the Committee might interview Hereros there; the Committee had been invited to conduct similar interviews in other African countries who had received refugees from the territory. The British offer, however, was made conditional on the Committee's assurance that it would make no unauthorized visit to the disputed territory, and was withdrawn when this was not forthcoming. South Africa made it plain that she would meet with force any attempts at illegal entry, and the visit was abandoned. Instead the Committee interviewed political refugees in Dar-es-Salaam and Cairo, and from this and the evidence of petitioners compiled a special report on conditions in South West Africa.

This Special Report of the Committee on South West Africa reported that South Africa was the only state in the world that still practised racism as official policy. It noted that

that policy was also being extended to South West Africa against the wishes of the native inhabitants. It asked the General Assembly to undertake a study of the ways and means of terminating the South West Africa mandate and of having its administration assumed directly or indirectly by the United Nations. The Committee expressed grave concern at South Africa's continued defiance of the authority of the United Nations, and urged that the organization establish its presence in South West Africa immediately. There were also allegations, based on the evidence taken in Africa, of militarization of the territory and that the situation threatened international peace and security.[7]

South Africa had won a diplomatic victory in the abandonment of the Committee's intention to try to visit South West Africa. However, there were signs of unrest both within South West Africa and in neighbouring territories, and moreover, having become a Republic and left the Commonwealth in May 1961, South Africa had lost moral—and sometimes diplomatic —support from many of its members. She therefore began to feel some need to appease the United Nations to some extent. This was reflected in her offer in November 1961 to invite three past presidents of the General Assembly to visit South West Africa in their personal capacities, to see for themselves whether there was any truth in the allegations about military terrorization, the existence of an explosive situation and the planned extermination of the native inhabitants.[8] Their views were to be reported not to the United Nations but to the South African Government, which undertook to publish them in full. The selection of the three past presidents was to be made by the South African Government in agreement with the president of the General Assembly.

Prolonged debate in the General Assembly, with most delegations opposed to this proposal, culminated in the establishment of a Special Committee for South West Africa (replacing the Committee on South West Africa, which was dissolved) consisting of seven members nominated by the president of the General Assembly.[9] Its task was to achieve, in consultation with South Africa, the following objectives:

(a) a visit to the territory of South West Africa before 1 May 1962;

(b) the evacuation from the territory of all military forces of the Republic of South Africa;

(c) the release of all political prisoners without distinction as to party or race;

(d) the repeal of all laws or regulations confining the indigenous inhabitants in reserves and denying them all freedom of movement, expression and association, and of all other laws and regulations which establish and maintain the intolerable system of *apartheid*;

(e) preparations for general elections to the Legislative Assembly, based on universal adult suffrage, to be held as soon as possible under the supervision and control of the United Nations;

(f) advice and assistance to the Government resulting from the general elections, with a view to preparing the territory for full independence;

(g) co-ordination of the economic and social assistance with which the Specialized Agencies will provide the people in order to promote their moral and material welfare;

(h) the return to the territory of indigenous inhabitants without risk of imprisonment, detention or punishment of any kind because of their political activities in or outside the territory.

In March 1962 the president of the General Assembly nominated the Governments of Brazil, Burma, Mexico, Norway, the Philippines, Somalia and Togo as members of the Special Committee for South West Africa.[10] Its first task, for which it sought South African co-operation, was to make a visit to the territory. The South African Government accordingly invited the Committee's chairman and vice-chairman, Mr Victorio Carpio of the Philippines and Dr Martinez de Alva of Mexico, to visit South West Africa to acquaint themselves with the territory and its peoples. To invite the whole Committee, South Africa felt, might prejudice her position in the case before the International Court, but she was prepared to discuss the matter at issue informally.

When, however, after a ten-day visit to South West Africa the two-man mission issued a joint communiqué with the South African Government in May 1962, the two agents of the United Nations stated that they had found neither evidence of genocide in South West Africa nor of militarization of the territory in violation of the terms of the mandate, and that there was no threat to international peace and security arising from South Africa's administration of the territory.[11] This disposed convincingly of the most serious allegations against South Africa, but temporized on a number of others, making no mention of the central issue of *apartheid*. Mr Carpio, in hospital at the later stages of the talks with the South African Government, repudiated the communiqué, though not until three weeks after its issue;[12] before Dr Alva could comment on this his Government had also disowned it.[13]

The chairman and vice-chairman of the Special Committee for South West Africa reported to the Committee in July 1962 that:

(a) the administration of the mandated territory was pervaded by the rigorous application of *apartheid*;

(b) the South African Government's policies, methods and objectives in administering the territory were in utter contradiction with the principles and purposes of the mandate, the United Nations Charter, the Universal Declaration of Human Rights and the enlightened conscience of mankind;

(c) South Africa had revealed no plans to institute reforms or relent from its policies and methods and was not developing the territory and its peoples for self-government or independence;

(d) it was the overwhelming desire of the African population that the United Nations assume direct administration of the territory and take all preparatory steps to grant freedom to the indigenous population as soon as possible;

(e) the attention of the General Assembly be drawn to the imperative need for continued firm action on the question by giving the South African Government a short period within which to comply with the General Assembly resolutions or, failing that, by considering the feasibility of revoking the mandate and simultaneously assuming the administration of the territory, if need be, by imposing sanctions or employing other means to enforce compliance with its decisions or resolutions.

The report, which mentioned nothing of the controversial communiqué, was adopted by the Special Committee as apt and timely.[14] The Committee pretended that there was no authentic communiqué, explaining that it had not been an official authorized act of the Committee and was therefore not binding.[15] The South African Government naturally protested.[16]

The whole episode had discredited and embarrassed not only the Committee but also the petitioners on South West Africa, the United Nations as a whole and the Afro-Asian countries in particular. And it had put United Nations unity in doubt.

Debating the report, the General Assembly expressed deep concern that the continuance of the critical situation in South West Africa constituted a threat to international peace and security, and reaffirmed its solemn proclamation that the people of South West Africa had an inalienable right to independence and national sovereignty.[17] It then dissolved the Special Committee for South West Africa, entrusting its work to the Special Committee of 17, which deals with the granting of independence to colonial countries and peoples.[18]

Although the Nationalist Government in South Africa has consistently maintained that the mandate for South West Africa, and South Africa's obligations there, expired with the League, South Africa has admitted that the territory has an 'international character', both overtly and implicitly in various actions as seen in earlier chapters. She is, however, unshakeably determined on applying there her policy of *apartheid* (in which she has complete faith), which the United Nations claims violates the mandate and the United Nations Charter. A consequence of the generally admitted 'international character' of the territory is that the United Nations should thus concern itself with the issue of racial policy, which in today's climate of opinion has become the crux of the dispute.

The eventual aim of the United Nations, or at least of the Afro-Asian members, is to end the mandate, either by transferring it to another administering power or by granting independence. The fate of the territory depends upon the outcome of the present case before the International Court, brought by Ethiopia and Liberia against South Africa. This case apparently now rests primarily upon obtaining a confirmation of the Advisory Opinion of 1950 and upon a judgment that the United Nations has inherited the authority of the League.

Should the Court uphold its earlier judgment, the United Nations resolutions against *apartheid*, and in respect of South West Africa, would presumably have added authority. In particular, the chief world powers might then be placed in a position where they had to make a public decision whether or not to support measures against South Africa. Although South Africa has been, and would doubtless continue to be, unwilling to conform to the pressure of world opinion on the South West Africa issue, it is not certain that South Africa would openly resist, in the first stages, a Court decision that upheld the transmission of the League's authority to the United Nations to be exercised in the spirit of the mandate. Nor is it certain that the Hague Court decision would mean the end of litigation: the Court might be asked to explain its findings and later, if United Nations action was contemplated, the legal interpretation of the articles under which it was to operate might be queried.

Whatever the International Court's decision, it is unlikely to prove more than the next step in the evolution of an international problem. But it may mark an important stage in the confrontation of South Africa, nationalist Africa and Asia, and the world powers.

APPENDIX I

Article 22 of the League of Nations Covenant

1. To those colonies and territories which as a consequence of the late war have ceased to be under the sovereignty of the States which formerly governed them and which are inhabited by peoples not yet able to stand by themselves under the strenuous conditions of the modern world, there should be applied the principle that the well-being and development of such peoples form a sacred trust of civilization and that securities for the performance of this trust should be embodied in this Covenant.

2. The best method of giving practical effect to this principle is that the tutelage of such peoples should be entrusted to advanced nations who, by reason of their resources, their experience or their geographical position, can best undertake this responsibility, and who are willing to accept it, and this tutelage should be exercised by them as Mandatories on behalf of the League.

3. The character of the Mandate must differ according to the stage of the development of the people, the geographical situation of the territory, its economic conditions and other similar circumstances.

4. Certain communities formerly belonging to the Turkish Empire have reached a stage of development where their existence as independent nations can be provisionally recognized subject to the rendering of administrative advice and assistance by a Mandatory until such time as they are able to stand alone. The wishes of these communities must be a principal consideration in the selection of the Mandatory.

5. Other peoples, especially those of Central Africa, are at such a stage that the Mandatory must be responsible for the

administration of the territory under the conditions which will guarantee freedom of conscience and religion, subject only to the maintenance of public order and morals, the prohibition of abuses such as the slave trade, the arms traffic and the liquor traffic, and the prevention of the establishment of fortifications or military and naval bases and of military training of the natives for other than police purposes and the defence of the territory, and will also secure equal opportunities for the trade and commerce of other members of the League.

6. There are territories, such as South West Africa and certain of the South Pacific Islands, which, owing to the sparseness of their population or their small size, or their remoteness from the centres of civilization, or their geographical contiguity to the territory of the Mandatory, and other circumstances, can be best administered under the laws of the Mandatory as integral portion of its territory, subject to the safeguards above mentioned in the interests of the indigenous population.

7. In every case of Mandate, the Mandatory shall render to the Council an annual report in reference to the territory committed to its charge.

8. The degree of authority, control or administration to be exercised by the Mandatory shall, if not previously agreed upon by the members of the League, be explicitly defined in each case by the Council.

9. A permanent Commission shall be constituted to receive and examine the annual reports of the Mandatories, and to advise the Council on all matters relating to the observance of the mandates.

APPENDIX II

The Mandate for South West Africa

The Council of the League of Nations,

Whereas by Article 19 of the treaty of peace with Germany, signed at Versailles on 28th June, 1919, Germany renounced in favour of the Principal Allied and Associated Powers all her rights over her overseas possessions, including therein German South West Africa, and

Whereas the Principal Allied and Associated Powers agreed that, in accordance with Article 2, Part I (Covenant of the League of Nations) of the said Treaty a Mandate should be conferred upon his Britannic Majesty to be exercised on his behalf by the Government of the Union of South Africa to administer the Territory aforementioned, and have proposed that the Mandate should be formulated in the following terms, and,

Whereas His Britannic Majesty, for and on behalf of the Government of the Union of South Africa has agreed to accept the Mandate in respect of the said territory, and has undertaken to exercise it on behalf of the League of Nations in accordance with the following provisions; and

Whereas, by the aforementioned Article 22, paragraph 8, it is provided that the degree of authority, control, or administration agreed upon by the members of the League, shall be explicitly defined by the Council of the League of Nations.

Confirming the said Mandate, defines its terms as follows:

Article 1

The territory over which a Mandate is conferred upon His Britannic Majesty for and on behalf of the Government of the Union of South Africa (hereinafter called the Mandatory) comprises the territory which formerly constituted the German Protectorate of South West Africa.

Article 2

The Mandatory shall have full power of administration and legislation over the territory subject to the present Mandate as an integral portion of the Union of South Africa, and may apply the laws of the Union of South Africa to the Territory, subject to such local modifications as circumstances may require.

The Mandatory shall promote to the utmost the material and moral well-being and the social progress of the inhabitants of the Territory, subject to the Present Mandate.

Article 3

The Mandatory shall see that the slave trade is prohibited, and that no forced labour is permitted except for essential public works and services, and then only for adequate remuneration.

The Mandatory shall also see that the traffic in arms and ammunition is controlled in accordance with principles analogous to those laid down in the Convention relating to the control of the arms traffic, signed on 10th September, 1919, or in any convention amending the same.

The supply of intoxicating spirits and beverages to the natives shall be prohibited.

Article 4

The military training of the natives, otherwise than for purposes of internal police and local defence of the Territory, shall be prohibited. Furthermore, no military or naval bases shall be established or fortifications erected in the Territory.

Article 5

Subject to the provisions of any local law for the maintenance of public order and public morals, the Mandatory shall ensure in the Territory freedom of conscience and the free exercise of all forms of worship and shall allow all missionaries, nationals of any state, members of the League of Nations, to enter into, travel, and reside in the Territory for the purpose of prosecuting their calling.

Article 6

The Mandatory shall make to the Council of the League of Nations an annual report to the satisfaction of the Council, containing full information with regard to the Territory, and indicating the measures taken to carry out the obligations assumed under Articles 2, 3, 4, and 5.

Article 7

The consent of the Council of the League of Nations is required for any modifications of the terms of the present Mandate.

The Mandatory agrees that, if any dispute whatever should arise between the Mandatory and another member of the League of Nations relating to the interpretation of the application of the provisions of the Mandate, such dispute, if it cannot be settled by negotiation, shall be submitted to the Permanent Court of International Justice, provided for by Article 14 of the Covenant of the League of Nations.

The present declaration shall be deposited in the Archives of the League of Nations. Certified copies shall be forwarded by the Secretary-General of the League of Nations to all Powers Signatories of the Treaty of Peace with Germany.

Made at Geneva, the 17th day of December, 1920.

APPENDIX III

United Nations Charter, Chapter XII:
International Trusteeship System, Articles 75–80

1. *Article 75*

    The United Nations shall establish under its authority an international trusteeship system for the administration and supervision of such territories as may be placed thereunder by subsequent individual agreements. These territories are hereinafter referred to as trust territories.

2. *Article 76*

    The basic objectives of the trusteeship system, in accordance with the purposes of the United Nations laid down in Article I of the present Charter, shall be:

    (a) to further international peace and security;

    (b) to promote the political, economic, social and educational advancement of the inhabitants of the trust territories, and their progressive development towards self-government or independence as may be appropriate to the particular circumstances of each territory and its peoples and the freely expressed wishes of the peoples concerned, and as may be provided by the terms of each trusteeship agreement;

    (c) to encourage respect for human rights and for fundamental freedoms for all without distinction as to race, sex, language, or religion, and to encourage recognition of the interdependence of the peoples of the world; and

    (d) to ensure equal treatment in social, economic, and commercial matters for all Members of the United Nations and their nationals, and also equal treatment for the latter in the administration of justice, without prejudice to the attainment of the foregoing objectives and subject to the provisions of Article 80.

3. *Article 77*

I. The trusteeship system shall apply to such territories in the following categories as may be placed thereunder by means of trusteeship agreements:

- (*a*) territories now held under mandate;
- (*b*) territories which may be detached from enemy States as a result of the Second World War; and
- (*c*) territories voluntarily placed under the system by States responsible for their administration.

II. It will be a matter for subsequent agreement as to which territories in the foregoing categories will be brought under the trusteeship system and upon what terms.

4. *Article 78*

The trusteeship system shall not apply to territories which have become Members of the United Nations, relationship among which shall be based on respect for the principle of sovereign equality.

5. *Article 79*

The terms of trusteeship for each territory to be placed under the trusteeship system, including any alteration or amendment, shall be agreed upon by the States directly concerned, including the mandatory power in the case of territories held under mandate by a Member of the United Nations, and shall be approved as provided for in Articles 83 and 85.

6. *Article 80*

I. Except as may be agreed upon in individual trusteeship agreements, made under Articles 77, 79, and 81, placing each territory under the trusteeship system, and until such agreements have been concluded, nothing in this Chapter shall be construed in or of itself to alter in any manner the rights whatsoever of any States or any peoples or the terms of existing international instruments to which Members of the United Nations may respectively be parties.

II. Paragraph I of this Article shall not be interpreted as giving grounds for delay or postponement of the negotiation and conclusion of agreements for placing mandated and other territories under the trusteeship system as provided for in Article 77.

SELECT BIBLIOGRAPHY

R. S. Baker, *Woodrow Wilson and World Settlement* (New York, Doubleday, Page and Co., 1922), Vol. I.

Ronald B. Ballinger, *South West Africa: The Case Against the Union* (Johannesburg, South African Institute of Race Relations, 1961).

G. L. Beer, *African Questions at the Paris Peace Conference* (New York, The Macmillan Company, 1923).

G. M. Carter, *The Politics of Inequality: South Africa since 1948* (London, Thames and Hudson, 1958; Praeger, New York, 1958).

B. T. G. Chidzero, *Tanganyika and International Trusteeship* (London and New York, Oxford University Press, 1961).

R. N. Chowdhuri, *International Mandates and the Trusteeship System: A Comparative Study* (The Hague, Martinus Nijhoff, 1955).

C. Dundas, *South West Africa: The Factual Background* (Johannesburg, South African Institute of Race Relations, 1946).

L. M. Goodrich and E. Hambro, *Charter of the United Nations: Commentary and Documents* (Boston, Mass., World Peace Foundation, 1946).

Lord Hailey (ed.), *An African Survey* (London and New York, Oxford University Press for the Royal Institute of International Affairs, revised ed., 1957).

J. D. Rheinallt Jones, *The Future of South West Africa* (Johannesburg, South African Institute of Race Relations, 1946).

A. Keppell-Jones, *South Africa: A Short History* (London, Hutchinson University Library, 1961).

R. Lansing, *The Peace Negotiations: A Personal Narrative* (London, Constable and Co., 1921).

League of Nations, *The Aims, Methods and Activity of the League of Nations* (Geneva, League Secretariat, 1938).

League of Nations, *The Mandates System: Origin—Principles—Application* (Geneva, League Secretariat, 1945).

R. W. Logan, *The Operation of the Mandate System in Africa, 1919–1927* (Washington, D.C., The Foundation Publishers, 1942).

R. W. Logan, *The African Mandate in World Politics* (Washington, D.C., Public Affairs Press, 1948).

Neil Macaulay, *Mandates, Reasons, Results, Remedies* (London, Methuen and Co., 1937).

Aaron M. Margalitti, *The International Mandates* (London, Oxford University Press, 1930).

Leo Marquard, *The Peoples and Policies of South Africa* (London, Oxford University Press, 1952; New York, Oxford University Press, 1963).

D. H. Miller, *The Drafting of the Covenant* (New York, G. P. Putnam and Sons, 1928), Vol. I.

James N. Murray, Jr, *The United Nations Trusteeship System* (Urbana, University of Illinois Press, 1957).

G. Heaton Nicholls, *South Africa in My Time* (London, George Allen and Unwin, 1961).

Karl F. Nowak, trans. N. Thomas and E. W. Dickes, *Versailles* (London, Victor Gollancz, 1928).

W. E. Rappard, *International Problems as Viewed from Geneva* (New Haven, Yale University Press, 1925).

Report on the Natives of South West Africa and their Treatment of Germany (London, H.M.S.O., 1918).

Charles Seymour, *The Intimate Papers of Colonel House: Vol. IV, The Ending of the War, June 1918–November 1919* (London, Ernest Benn, 1928).

J. C. Smuts, *The League of Nations: A Practical Suggestion* (London, Hodder and Stoughton, 1918).

South West Africa and South Africa: The History of a Mandate (New York, published by the authority of the South African Government, 1946).

United Nations, *A Sacred Trust: The Work of the United Nations for Dependent Peoples* (New York, U.N. Publications, 1951).

Campbell L. Upthegrove, *Empire by Mandate* (New York, Record Press, 1954).

Eric A. Walker, *A History of Southern Africa* (London and New York, Longmans, Green and Co., 1957).

Quincy Wright, *Mandates under the League of Nations* (Illinois, University of Chicago Press, 1930).

References

1. The Establishment of the Mandate

[1] *British and Foreign State Papers*, Vol. 106, p. 953.

[2] Frank Cobb and Walter Lippmann quoted in Charles Seymour, *The Intimate Papers of Colonel House* (London and New York, 1928), Vol. III, p. 953.

[3] Ibid., p. 57.

[4] Ibid., Vol. IV, 1928, pp. 152–3.

[5] *British and Foreign State Papers*, Vol. III, pp. 960–1: Address to both Houses of Congress on 'Principles for Establishment of Peace'.

[6] David Hunter Miller, *The Drafting of the Covenant* (New York, 1928), Vol. II, p. 88.

[7] Hansard, *Parliamentary History*, Vol. 23, Cols. 1316–17.

[8] R. S. Baker, *Woodrow Wilson and World Settlement* (New York, Doubleday, Page and Co., 1922), Vol. I, p. 263.

[9] J. C. Smuts, *The League of Nations: A Practical Suggestion* (London, Hodder and Stoughton, 1918), pp. 11–12, 15, 17, 21–3.

[10] Ibid., p. 15.

[11] Karl Friederich Nowak, *Versailles* (London, Gollancz, 1928), p. 48.

[12] Campbell L. Upthegrove, *Empire by Mandate* (New York, Record Press, 1954), p. 25.

[13] *Foreign Relations of the United States*, op. cit., Vol. III, pp. 719–723, 740–3.

[14] Quoted in R. W. Logan, *The Operation of the Mandate System in Africa, 1919–1927* (Washington, D.C., The Foundation Publishers, 1942), p. 13.

[15] *The Drafting of the Covenant*, Vol. I, p. 368.

[16] PMC Minutes, 20th Session, 1931, CPM 1183, Annex 3 (a), p. 196.

[17] Ibid., pp. 195–6.

[18] For a description of the Permanent Mandates Commission, see Chapter 2, note 1 (p. 75).

[19] *The Drafting of the Covenant*, Vol. I, p. 188.

[20] League of Nations Official Journal (LNOJ), Special Supplement No. 81, 10th Assembly, 6th Committee, 1929, p. 20.

2. *The Administration of the Trust under the League of Nations*

[1] The Permanent Mandates Commission was originally composed of nine members chosen for their competence and in their personal capacity from Portugal, France, the United Kingdom, Holland, Italy, Sweden, Japan, Belgium and Spain. It was later enlarged to include M. Rappard (Switzerland) in 1925 and a German in 1927.

[2] Treaty of Peace with Germany, 1919, Articles 23, 119, 122, 127, 257, 278.

[3] International Court of Justice (ICJ) (Reports): *International Status of South West Africa*, 1950, p. 132.

[4] PMC Minutes, 26th Session, 1934, p. 51; LNOJ Special Supplement No. 84, Sept. 1930, p. 54; PMC Minutes, 27th Session, 1935, p. 239.

[5] PMC Minutes, 18th Session, 1930, p. 145, for statement by Mr Courtney Clarke, Assistant Secretary of the Administration of South West Africa.

[6] Special Supplement No. 23, 1924, p. 128.

[7] Speeches by Haitian and Indian delegates, 2nd and 3rd Assemblies, Plenary Meetings, 1921, p. 352, and Vol. I, p. 155.

[8] PMC Minutes, 11th Session, 1927.

[9] Ibid.

[10] PMC Minutes, 14th Session, 1928.

[11] PMC Minutes, 9th Session, 1926, p. 35.

[12] PMC Minutes, 2nd Session, 1922, p. 37; a criticism reiterated by the Indian delegate at the 3rd League Assembly.

[13] The remarks of the Marquis Theodoli, the first Chairman, in PMC Minutes, 3rd Session, 1923, p. 105.

[14] PMC Minutes, 27th Session, 1935, p. 163.

[15] PMC Minutes, 1st Session, 1921, p. 41.

[16] For discussions on this issue see PMC Minutes, 1st Session, 1921, p. 41; 2nd Session, 1921, p. 27; 3rd Session, 1923, pp. 61, 111; 6th Session, 1925, pp. 72–6; 9th Session, 1926, pp. 41, 220; 11th Session, 1927, p. 205; 14th Session, 1928, pp. 83, 275; 18th Session, 1930, pp. 135–9; 20th Session, 1931, p. 66; 22nd Session, 1932, pp. 34–5; 23rd Session, 1933, p. 93; 26th Session, 1934, pp. 54–8; 27th Session, 1935, pp. 162–6; 29th Session, 1936, pp. 136, 212;

31st Session, 1937, pp. 118–30; 34th Session, 1938, p. 91; 36th Session, 1939, p. 32.

[17] Administration of South West Africa: *Report of the Commission of Inquiry into Non-European Education in South West Africa*, 1958, pp. 82–4, 87 and 93.

[18] PMC Minutes, 3rd Session, 1923, pp. 203, 205–6, 293.

[19] LNOJ Special Supplement No. 33, 1925, p. 106; No. 39, 1925, p. 23; PMC Minutes, 6th Session, 1925, p. 62.

[20] LNOJ, 10th Year, No. 11, 1929, p. 1467; LNOJ, 11th Year, No. 2, 1930, p. 70.

[21] PMC, 6th Session, 1925, p. 64; see also LNOJ, 7th Year, No. 7, p. 867.

[22] LNOJ, 11th Year, No. 7, 1930, p. 839.

[23] PMC Minutes, 2nd Session, 1922, Annex 6, p. 91.

[24] Ibid., Annex 4, pp. 86–7.

[25] PMC Minutes, 9th Session, 1926, p. 35.

3. South West Africa and Union–German Relations

[1] LN Doc. C 257, 1923 VI; OJ, 4th Year, No. 6, 1923, Annex 497, pp. 658–9; PMC Minutes, 2nd Session, 1922, Annex 4, pp. 86–7; 16th Session, 1929, Annex 8 (B) pp. 129, 189–90.

[2] PMC Minutes, 36th Session, 1939, p. 19.

[3] PMC Minutes, 33rd Session, 1937, p. 146, for Dr Hirsehorn's allegations, and cf. Professor Eric A. Walker, *A History of Southern Africa* (London and New York, Longmans, Green, 1957), p. 614.

[4] See PMC Minutes, 26th Session, 1934, p. 50, for text of the resolution to this effect by the South West Africa Legislative Assembly, reported in the *Windhoek Advertiser* of 6 June 1934.

[5] PMC Minutes, 27th Session, 1935, p. 161.

4. From the League to the United Nations

[1] LNOJ, General, Series I, 1946, p. 73.

[2] Ibid., p. 68.

[3] PMC Minutes, 20th Session, 1931, Annex 16, p. 229; LNOJ, 12th Year, No. 11, Council Minutes, 1931, p. 2057.

[4] Ibid., p. 2051.

[5] UN General Assembly Official Records, 1st Session, 1st Part, 12th Plenary Meeting, 1946, p. 591.

[6] Ibid., pp. 185–6.

[7] UNGAOR, 2nd Part, 1st Session, 4th Committee, 1946, pp. 199–235. Doc. A/123, Annex 13.

[8] Ibid.

[9] Rt. Hon. G. H. Nicholls, pp. 399, 401; SA, H. of A. Deb. Vol. 60, 1947, Cols. 1342–3.

[10] SA, Votes and Proceedings of the H. of A., 9th Parliament, 4th Session, 1947, p. 149, motion by Mr Eric Louw.

[11] SA, H. of A. Deb., Vol. 60, 1947, Col. 1329.

[12] UN Doc. A/C/4/45; GAOR, 2nd Part, 1st Session, 4th Committee, Part I, 1946, pp. 69–71.

[13] UN Doc. A/C4/345, 51, 58, 61, GAOR, 4th Committee, 15th, 17th, 19th and 20th Meetings, November 1946, pp. 73, 84, 97–8 and 108 respectively.

[14] UN Doc. A/C4/51, 58, GAOR, 4th Committee, November 1946, pp. 86–7, 99 ff., 103.

[15] UN Doc. A/C4/57, GAOR, 2nd Part, 1st Session, 4th Committee, 1946, Annex 11, p. 188.

[16] Leo Marquard, *The Peoples and Politics of South Africa* (London, Oxford University Press, 1952; New York, 1963), p. 224.

[17] See *New York Times*, 29 October 1946.

[18] UN Doc. A/C4/58, GAOR, 4th Committee, 1946, pp. 101–3.

5. South West Africa and the United Nations 1946–53

[1] UN Doc. A/334, GAOR, 2nd Session, 4th Committee, 1947, pp. 133–6.

[2] Ibid., p. 16.

[3] UNGAOR, 2nd Session, Plenary Meetings, Vol. I, 1947, pp. 597, 600.

[4] The following states held that the Charter imposed a legal obligation: India, China, USSR, Byelorussia, Poland, Philippines, Guatemala, Uruguay, Columbia, Syria, Haiti, Brazil.

[5] The following States held that the Charter did not impose a legal obligation: United Kingdom, Netherlands, United States, Cuba, Australia, Union of South Africa, Denmark, France, Greece, New Zealand, Belgium, Canada, Bolivia, Iraq.

[6] Ibid., p. 578.

[7] UN Doc. A/C4/57, Annex II, GAOR, 1st Session, 2nd Part, 4th Committee, 1946, p. 188.

[8] UNGAOR, 2nd Session, Vol. I, Plenary Meetings, 1947, p. 581; UNCIO Doc. 448, II/4/21, Vol. X, pp. 459–60; Doc. 512 II/4/21, pp. 468–70.

[9] UNGAOR, 2nd Session, Vol. I, Plenary Meetings, 1947, pp. 591, 593, 604–5.

[10] UN, Yearbook of the United Nations, 1947–8, pp. 143–4.

[11] UNGAOR, 2nd Session, 4th Committee, 1947, pp. 16–45, 48–50, 64–70; 2nd Session, Vol. I, Plenary Meetings, 1947, pp. 627–637.

[12] UN Doc. A/603, pp. 43–5; Yearbook of the United Nations, 1947–8, pp. 783–6.

[13] UNGAOR, 4th Session, 4th Committee, 1949, pp. 201–2.

[14] UNGAOR, 4th Session, 4th Committee, 1948, p. 203; and Plenary Meeting, 1949, p. 523.

[15] UN, Yearbook of the United Nations, 1948–9, p. 870.

[16] UN Doc. A/C4/4.66 (a)–(h):

(a) Petition of the Herero tribe to the United Nations.
(b) Letter from Chief Hosea Kutako and five other members of the Herero tribe.
(c) Statement by Chief David Wibooi of the Nama tribe.
(d) Statement by eleven members of the Nama tribe.
(e) Statements pertaining to the dispossession of the tribesmen of their land.
(f) Statements pertaining to labour conditions on farms.
(g) Extract from the report of the South West Africa Natives Labourers' Commission, 1945–8.
(h) The South West Africa Referendum.

[17] UNGAOR, 4th Session, Plenary Meetings, 1949, pp. 44–5.

[18] ICJ (Reports): *International Status of South West Africa*, 1950.

[19] UN, Yearbook of the United Nations, 1950, p. 820.

[20] Ibid., 1951, p. 631.

[21] UN Doc. A/2261, GAOR, 7th Session, Annexes, 1958.

6. South West Africa and the United Nations 1953–61

[1] UN Doc. A/2630, GAOR, 8th Session, Supp. 17, 1953, pp. 26–7.

[2] UN Doc. A/L.178 as GA Res. 904 (IX) of 23 November 1954.

[3] ICJ (Reports), *Voting Procedure on South West Africa*, 1955, p. 94.

[4] UN Doc A/C4/L.405 as GA Res. 934 (X) of 3 December 1955.

[5] LNOJ No. 4, 1927, Annex 938, p. 438.

[6] LNOJ, No. 12, 1926, pp. 1646–53; No. 3, pp. 314–15.

[7] Ibid., No. 4, p. 438.

[8] UN Doc. A/2913/Add. 2.

[9] UN Doc. A/3116: GAOR, 10th Session, Supp. 19, 1955, pp. 19–24.

[10] ICJ (Reports), *South West Africa (Hearings of Petitioners)*, 1956, p. 27.

[11] UNGAOR, 4th Committee, 10th Session, 1955, p. 182.

[12] UN, Yearbook of the United Nations, 13th Session, 1958, p. 313.

[13] Ibid., 14th Session, 1959, p. 323; 15th Session, 1960, pp. 490–492; 16th Session, 1961, p. 461.

[14] UN Doc. A/2666, Supp. 14, 1954, Report of the Committee on South West Africa, p. 31.

[15] Annual reports submitted by the Committee on South West Africa to the General Assembly:

1954: UN Doc. A/2666,	9th Session,		Supp. 14.	
1955: „ „ A/2913,	10th	„	„	12.
1956: „ „ A/3151,	11th	„	„	12.
1957: „ „ A/3626,	12th	„	„	12.
1958: „ „ A/3906,	13th	„	„	12.
1959: „ „ A/4191,	14th	„	„	12.
1960: „ „ A/4464,	15th	„	„	12.
1961: „ „ A/4957,	16th	„	„	12.

[16] UN Doc. A/3541.

[17] UN Doc. A/3625, GAOR, 12th Session, 1957, Supp. 12a.

[18] UN Doc. A/C4/L.447, Yearbook of the United Nations, 11th Session, 1956, p. 308.

[19] UN Docs. A/C4/L.492 and 495; GA Res. 1143 (XII).

[20] UN Doc. A/3900, Yearbook of the United Nations, 13th Session, 1958, pp. 312–14 and 317; report of the Committee.

[21] UN Doc. A/4957, Yearbook of the United Nations, 16th Session, 1961, p. 458.

[22] UN Doc. A/4926, Yearbook of the United Nations, 1961, pp. 455–9.

[23] UN Docs. A/C4/L.533, 595, 653, 714; 1958–61.

7. *A New Era: from 1960*

[1] UN, Yearbook of the United Nations, 15th Session, 1960, p. 492.

[2] UN Doc. A/C4/L.655, GA Res. 1566 (XV), 954th plenary meeting.

[3] *The Times* (London), 5 November 1960, p. 6, col. 5.

[4] ICJ (Reports): *Ethiopia* v. *South Africa, Liberia* v. *South Africa* (originally separate identical submissions, so reckoned as one party).

[5] UN, Yearbook of the United Nations, 17th Session, 1962, pp. 469–72.

[6] ICJ Reports, *South West Africa Cases* (*Ethiopia* v. *South Africa, Liberia* v. *South Africa*) (*Preliminary Objections*), 1962, pp. 319–662.

[7] UN Doc. A/4926.

[8] UN, Yearbook of the United Nations, 16th Session, 1961, p. 461.

[9] UN Doc. A/5044 adopted as GA Res. 1702 (XVI) on 19 December 1961.

[10] UN, Yearbook of the United Nations, 16th Session, 1961, p. 463.

[11] *Sunday Telegraph* (London), 27 May 1962, p. 19.

[12] *Daily Telegraph* (London), 25 July 1962, p. 22, col. 5.

[13] Ibid.

[14] UN, Yearbook of the United Nations, 17th Session, 1962, p. 440.

[15] Ibid., pp. 440–1.

[16] UN Doc. A/AC/110/8.

[17] UN Doc. A/5310, GA Res. 1805 (XVII), December 1962.

[18] UN Doc. A/C4/L.757, GA Res. 1806 (XVII), December 1962.